Essential Histories

The Second War of
Italian Unification 1859–61

Essential Histories

The Second War of
Italian Unification 1859–61

Frederick C. Schneid

Acknowledgments

I would like to thank Colonello Antonino Zarcone, Chief of the Ufficio Storico dello Stato Maggiore dell'Esercito, and Capitane di Vascello Francesco Loriga, Chief of the Ufficio Storico della Marina Militare, for their kindness and aid in their military archives. I would also like to thank my friend Ciro Paoletti for his support and encouragement of my research in Italian military history.

Editor's note

The French and Piedmontese armies possessed similar ranking systems. The Austrian Army, however, had distinct titles that do not necessarily translate as equivalents to those of their French or Piedmontese counterparts. The highest rank in the Austrian Army was Feldmarschall, followed by Feldzeugmeister for infantry, artillery, and engineers and General der Kavallerie for cavalry. Thereafter, it was Feldmarschall Leutnant and then General.

Except where noted, all quotations originally in languages other than English have been translated by the author.

On the maps in this volume, the divisional level of command on the Austrian side has been omitted for clarity. Most accounts refer to Austrian Korps and brigades rather than divisions.

First published in Great Britain in 2012 by Osprey Publishing, Midland House, West Way, Botley, Oxford, OX2 0PH, UK
44-02 23rd Street, Suite 219, Long Island City, NY 11101, USA

Email: info@ospreypublishing.com

Osprey Publishing is part of The Osprey Group

Print ISBN: 978 1 84908 787 2
PDF ebook ISBN: 978 1 84908 853 4
ePub ebook ISBN: 978 1 78096 450 8

Page layout by The Black Spot
Index by Fineline Editorial Services
Typeset in Gill Sans and ITC Stone Serif
Maps by Peter Bull Art Studio
Originated by PDQ Media, Bungay, UK
Printed in China through Bookbuilders

12 13 14 15 16   10 9 8 7 6 5 4 3 2 1

Osprey Publishing is supporting the Woodland Trust, the UK's leading woodland conservation charity, by funding the dedication of trees.

www.ospreypublishing.com

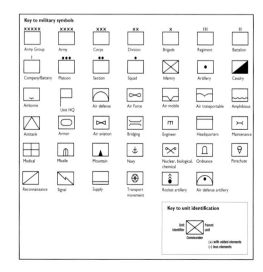

Contents

Introduction   7

Chronology   11

Background to war
The Risorgimento as war and revolution, 1815–49   13

Warring sides
The Italian Kingdoms, France, and Austria   21

Outbreak
Revolutions, plots, and planning   28

The fighting
The Second War of Italian Unification, 1859–61   34

Portrait of a soldier
Giuseppe Cesare Abba and Garibaldi's Thousand   71

The world around war
The threat of a general European war   74

Portrait of a civilian
An anonymous Neapolitan account   79

How the war ended
From Villafranca to Gaeta   82

Conclusion and consequences   87

Select bibliography   92

Index   94

Introduction

The Second War of Italian Unification (1859–61) was one of four such conflicts that led to the creation of modern Italy. The First War (1848–49) was an abject failure, but the subsequent conflict beginning in 1859 achieved unification. The war can be properly divided into three phases: the Franco-Piedmontese war with Austria, April–July 1859; Garibaldi's conquest of Sicily, May–August 1860; and the Piedmontese and Garibaldinian campaigns against Naples and the Papal States, September 1860–February 1861.

The Risorgimento, the movement that embodied revolutionary and nationalist aspirations in Italy during the 19th century, had suffered numerous failures prior to 1859, but its greatest success required the merging of liberal and conservative principles, with the support of foreign powers – notably France – to introduce a constitutional monarchy that presided over 85 percent of the Italian peninsula. This achievement was the product of calculating diplomacy directed by Camillo Benso, Count of Cavour, prime minister to Victor Emmanuel II, King of Piedmont–Sardinia. By no means did he work alone. Cavour's success was limited to northern and central Italy. The famed Italian revolutionary and general Giuseppe Garibaldi was responsible for the conquest of the south in 1860. Their cooperative military efforts led to the declaration of the Kingdom of Italy in March 1861.

Prince Clemens von Metternich, the Austrian Chancellor through 1848, famously said, "Italy is nothing but a geographic expression." His statement reflected the political reality that had existed in the Italian peninsula for more than a thousand years. By the late 18th century Italy comprised eight independent states: from north to south, the Kingdom of Piedmont–Sardinia, the Kingdom of Lombardy–Venetia, the duchies of Parma and Modena, the Grand Duchy of Tuscany, the Papal States and the Kingdom of Naples – this last also called the Kingdom of the Two Sicilies.

The independence of Italian politics ceased after 1494 when the French king Charles VIII invaded the peninsula to lay claim to the Kingdom of Naples. The Spanish responded with the dispatch of an army, and for the next three centuries Italy became a chessboard for European dynastic competition. The Spanish Habsburgs established their dominance by the mid-16th century. After the War of the Spanish Succession the Bourbons ascended the throne of Spain and subordinate branches of that house retained control of Parma and Modena until the French Revolution. The Austrian Habsburgs acquired Lombardy, Tuscany, and Naples in 1713. Venice's power had passed, chipped away by wars with the Turks. In 1738, the Bourbons reclaimed Naples and held it until 1861.

The House of Savoy, the rulers of the Duchy of Piedmont, held a special place within Italian politics. Piedmont's purpose within the context of dynastic competition was to keep the Habsburgs and Bourbons apart. Its rulers played a careful game, backing one, then the other, depending upon the circumstances. In 1721 Piedmont was joined with the Kingdom of Sardinia to form a new state. The House of Savoy became one of only two kingdoms in the peninsula. It retained its freedom of action through cautious diplomacy and the maintenance of a well-trained and disciplined army. Perhaps more important, Piedmont–Sardinia controlled the Alpine gate, the passes and their roads that ran between France and the north-Italian plain. Forts, strategically placed, established a clear frontier of power, although the Duchy of Savoy lay on the French side. To the east the kingdom bordered Austrian Lombardy defined by the Ticino River.

Between 1748 and 1792 Italy enjoyed a respite from European conflict, as an alliance between France and Austria neutralized the peninsula. Italian princes demobilized much

of their military power, reducing costs and pursuing domestic reforms. The Enlightenment held sway in much of Italy. Leopold of Tuscany (r. 1765–90) was perhaps one of the most progressive 18th-century princes. The rulers of Piedmont–Sardinia too

Risorgimento Italy, 1848–70

Legend:
- Kingdom of Piedmont–Sardinia
- Lombardy
- Venetia
- Duchy of Parma
- Duchy of Modena
- Papal States (to Piedmont–Sardinia 1860)
- Papal states (independent until 1870)
- Grand Duchy of Tuscany
- Kingdom of the Two Sicilies

o City
■ Fortress
Ⓐ Montebello, May 20, 1859
Ⓑ Palestro, May 30–31, 1859
Ⓒ Magenta, June 4, 1859
Ⓓ Solferino–San Martino, June 24, 1859
Ⓔ Calatafimi, May 15, 1860
Ⓕ Palermo, May 27–June 7, 1860
Ⓖ Milazzo, July 20, 1860
Ⓗ Pesaro, September 11, 1860
Ⓘ Spoleto, September 16–17, 1860
Ⓙ Castelfidardo, September 18, 1860
Ⓚ Volturno, October 1, 1860

0   100 miles
0   200 km

embraced reform. The French Revolutionary Wars, however, shattered this peaceful period.

The French invasion of Savoy and Nice in 1792 ushered in an era of dramatic change to Italian politics and society. Although, at this time, it is inappropriate to generalize a singular "Italian" culture, the French Revolutionary Wars impacted every corner of the peninsula. In 1796, General Napoleon Bonaparte's lightning campaign in northern Italy led to the collapse of Austrian military and political power. Napoleon formed the Cisalpine and Cispadane Republics during his year in Italy. Satellites of the French Republic, these states were administered by Italian revolutionaries sympathetic to the ideals of the revolution and decidedly opposed to the old regime and Austria. In 1802, Napoleon merged the states into the Italian Republic, and in 1804 he transformed it into the Kingdom of Italy, which ruled the north. The entire peninsula was impacted by Napoleonic rule as a result of the annexation of Piedmont (1802) and of Tuscany and the Papal States (1808) to Imperial France. The Kingdom of Naples came under French rule in 1806 with the ascent of Napoleon's sister and brother-in-law to the throne.

Napoleonic rule lasted until 1814 and its influence in Italy varied depending upon the state. Most of northern Italy was under French control for almost 20 years, while in the south it lasted for fewer than ten. Lombards formed the majority of the administration and military leadership in the Kingdom of Italy, as Piedmont was nothing more than an appendage of Napoleon's empire. The House of Savoy went into exile in Sardinia. The restoration of Italy to its pre-Napoleonic shape was formalized at the Congress of Vienna in 1814–15. The Bourbons returned to Naples in 1815, and the Habsburgs established direct control over Lombardy–Venetia, annexing the new kingdom to its greater empire.

Opposite: war and revolution in Italy during the 19th century revolved around the desire to establish constitutional governments and the unification of the peninsula. The process involved four wars between 1848 and 1870: three against Austria and the fourth to seize Rome.

Camillo Benso, Count of Cavour was one of the leading figures of the Risorgimento. He was a conservative nationalist and joined the administration of King Victor Emmanuel II, serving as minister of finance and then prime minister. He was the architect of Italian unification. (The Art Archive/Brera Library Milan/Collection Dagli Orti)

Subordinate houses were established in Tuscany, Parma, and Modena.

Historians continue to debate the extent of the impact of Napoleonic rule on Italy, but it is clear that the period marked a change in the trajectory of Italian history. After 1815, Italy experienced waves of revolution, which began as movements to establish constitutional governments, but eventually these aspirations acquired a nationalist tone. Liberals (the 19th-century term for constitutionalists) desired a unified state in the peninsula, exclusive of foreign powers. This meant revolutions to force Italian princes to accept constitutional limitations on their power, and equally the exclusion of Austria from Lombardy–Venetia. The first half of the 19th century in Italy therefore witnessed extensive Austrian military intervention to prevent revolutionaries from achieving their goals.

Among historians of Italy there are some who argue that the pursuit of revolutionary and nationalist agendas, the Risorgimento, was manufactured by a select few. The majority of Italians, the peasants and the day laborers, had little interest in a unified state even if they understood the benefits of a

Pope Pius IX (r. 1846–78) was initially sympathetic to constitutionalism in the Italian peninsula, but not in Rome. He was slow to institute reforms, and while giving his initial blessing to support the First War of Italian Unification, he eventually opposed it, leading to a revolution in Rome. He fled the city in 1849, restored only with the support of a French army. He presided over the Roman Catholic Church during the period of unification, 1859–70. (Library of Congress)

constitution. Furthermore, within the movements there was a clear division between constitutional monarchists and republicans. The *Carbonari*, the first revolutionaries in Italy, did not possess a clear nationalist agenda. Subsequently, Giuseppe Mazzini, the most ardent and influential revolutionary intellectual in Italy, began with more modest goals of establishing republican governments throughout the peninsula. Republicanism first and foremost was the basis of his political philosophy. The advent of Italian nationalism appeared in the wake of the failures of Mazzinianism to achieve victory. Vicenzo Gioberti, a former Mazzinian, argued that Italy could be free by looking to the "primacy of the Pope" to preside over a unified Italian state. Cesare Balbo and Camillo di Cavour disagreed, and in their newspaper, *Il Risorgimento*, advocated a federated Italy under the House of Savoy.

These disagreements between the Italian liberal and conservative nationalists represented an intellectual discourse. The achievement of unification in 1861 through Piedmontese action and the creation of a constitutional monarchy in the Kingdom of Italy appeared as an abandonment of Mazzinian principles and was rejected by some. Thus, the historiography (the study of how historians interpret history) of Italy in the 19th century includes those who reject the use of the term Risorgimento, because it implies a national consciousness that could not be found among the majority of Italians – peasants and the poor. Yet, the counter-argument proceeds, Italy was unified and therefore there was a Risorgimento. Whether the majority envisioned it in 1861 does not factor into the specific events that led to the creation of a unitary state.

Chronology

1796 Napoleon's conquest of northern
Italy; creation of Cisalpine Republic

1797 Creation of Cispadane Republic

1802 Creation of Italian Republic;
annexation of Piedmont to France

1804 Creation of Kingdom of Italy

1806 French conquest of Kingdom of
Naples

1808 Annexation of Tuscany and Papal
States to France

1814 Congress of Vienna, restoration of
-15 pre-Napoleonic borders; Austrian
annexation of Lombardy–Venetia

1820 Revolution in Naples

1821 Revolution in Piedmont; Austrian
military intervention; restoration of
monarchies in Naples and Piedmont

1830 Revolution in Parma, Modena, and
Papal States; Austrian military
intervention

1831 Charles Albert I ascends the throne in
Piedmont–Sardinia

1834 Mazzinian revolution in Piedmont
thwarted; Garibaldi flees to South
America

1848 Revolutions in Lombardy and
Venetia; revolution in France and
Austrian Empire; revolutions in
Tuscany, Modena, and Parma;
revolution in Sicily; First War of
Italian Unification; battles of
Pastrengo, Santa Lucia, Goito, and
Custozza; Franz Josef becomes
Emperor of Austria; Louis-Napoleon
Bonaparte elected President of the
Second French Republic

1849 Battle of Novara; abdication of
Charles Albert; accession of Victor
Emmanuel II; revolution in Rome;
Garibaldi's defense of the Roman
Republic; French siege of Rome;
Garibaldi's flight from Rome and exile

1851 Coup d'état in France ends Second
French Republic

1852 Camillo Benso, Count of Cavour,
appointed prime minister of
Piedmont–Sardinia; coronation of
Louis-Napoleon as Napoleon III,
Emperor of the French; creation of
Second French Empire

1854 General Alfonso La Marmora
institutes sweeping military reforms
in Piedmont–Sardinia; Crimean War
begins

1855 Piedmont–Sardinia joins British,
French, and Ottoman allies in
Crimean War

1856 Crimean War ends. Treaty of Paris

1858 Orsini bomb plot; secret agreement at
Plombières between Cavour and
Napoleon III

1859 **January** Secret military convention
between France and Piedmont–
Sardinia
April Austrian ultimatum to
Piedmont; Second War of Italian
Unification begins; Austrian army in
Lombardy invades Piedmont; France
enters war
May Battle of Montebello; battle of
Palestro
June Revolutions in Tuscany, Parma,
and Modena; battle of Magenta; battle
of Solferino and San Martino
July Peace of Villafranca
November Treaty of Zurich;
Lombardy transferred to France then
Piedmont

1860 **March** Tuscany, Parma, Modena,
Romagna, and Legations annexed to
Piedmont–Sardinia; Nice and Savoy
transferred to France
May Garibaldi's expedition to Sicily;
battle of Calatafimi; battle of Palermo
August Battle of Milazzo; Garibaldi
crosses Straits of Messina

The battle of Montebello was the first engagement of the Second War of Unification. Here, General Forey's division of I Corps run into elements of two Austrian corps sent across the Po to prevent a perceived French flank march. Forey's outnumbered battalions repelled the Austrian attacks. (Anne S.K. Brown Military Collection, Brown University Library)

September Garibaldi captures Naples; Piedmont invades Papal States; battle of Castelfidardo

October Battle of the Volturno; siege of Capua

November Siege of Gaeta begins

1861 **February** Gaeta surrenders; Francis II goes into exile; Kingdom of Naples annexed to Kingdom of Italy

March Victor Emmanuel II crowned Victor Emmanuel I of Italy; unification of Italy, excluding Rome and Venetia

1862 Cavour dies; Garibaldi attempts to seize Rome; battle of Aspromonte

1866 Italy joins Prussia in war against Austria; second battle of Custozza; annexation of Venetia by Kingdom of Italy

1867 Garibaldi attempts to seize Rome; battle of Mentana

1870 Franco-Prussian War; Italian troops storm Porto Pia capturing Rome; annexation of Rome completes unification of Italy

The Risorgimento as war and revolution, 1815–49

The concept of a unified Italy appeared during the 18th century, but the Napoleonic era provided practical experience in terms of an Italian administration and propaganda, which advanced the idea of an Italian national consciousness. The collapse of the Napoleonic regimes in the kingdoms of Italy and Naples, followed by the restoration of the Kingdom of Piedmont–Sardinia, removed French domination of the peninsula, but left in its wake a significant impact on those who supported the Napoleonic regimes and more importantly the notion of constitutional governments and an Italy devoid of foreign powers. Sympathy for these revolutionary ideals could be found in the armies of the respective Italian states, and the soldiers who had previously served their Napoleonic rulers. Those who supported the administrations, and the young raised during the Revolutionary–Napoleonic era, also sought change to the restored monarchies.

The *Carbonari*, formed in the immediate aftermath of the Napoleonic era, formed the first large-scale revolutionary movement in the peninsula. Although Naples was the center of *Carbonari* activity, similar organizations – *Rivendite* and *Federati* – emerged in Parma, Modena, Tuscany, and Piedmont. The *Carbonari* advocated the establishment of constitutional monarchy. In 1820, the *Carbonari* of Naples staged a revolution, supported by substantial elements of the Royal Army led by former Napoleonic general Guglielmo Pepe. Ferdinand IV, King of Naples (who would later be Ferdinand II, King of the Two Sicilies), feared that the rest of his army was disloyal and succumbed to revolutionary pressure. The king fled to Austria after accepting a constitution.

Clemens von Metternich, foreign minister of Austria, watched the Neapolitan revolution with great concern. He reestablished an

Giuseppe Mazzini founded Young Italy, which advocated republicanism and unification. Mazzinians rejected conservative nationalism, and sought to overthrow monarchical regimes, including the House of Savoy. Giuseppe Garibaldi was one of Mazzini's early followers. (Sailko)

Austrian presence in Italy in 1815, and went so far as to recommend creating an Italian Confederation under the direction of the King of Lombardy–Venetia (the Austrian emperor Francis I). His proposal was rejected at the Congress of Vienna, but the Austrian Habsburg dynasty presided over most of the states, and maintained an army in excess of 100,000 men in Italy. Metternich feared that the revolution in Naples would encourage others in the peninsula. With the support of the Russians, Prussians, and French, he issued the Troppau Protocols in 1821, which stated that revolution threatened the natural order and would be met by force. Metternich hoped that this warning would suffice to restore Ferdinand IV to full power and discourage further revolutions. His plan failed.

On March 11–12, 1821, the *Carbonari* in Piedmont, supported by eight regiments of infantry and cavalry, proclaimed a revolution. They demanded that King Victor Emmanuel I establish a constitution. The king abdicated and then fled, naming his brother Charles Felix as his successor. Charles Felix was not in Piedmont at the time, and his son Charles Albert was declared regent. The young prince accepted a constitution against his brother's wishes.

Metternich responded to events by dispatching the Austrian forces in Lombardy–Venetia to Piedmont and Naples. The Austrian army joined with Charles Felix's loyal regiments and made short work of the revolutionaries. Charles Albert was sent into temporary exile in France. The Austrian army in Naples crushed the *Carbonari* and the mutinous regiments, restoring Ferdinand IV. In both Piedmont and Naples the constitutions were abolished and the *Carbonari* brutally suppressed.

The failure of the revolutions of 1821 did not eliminate revolutionary sentiment in Italy. Giuseppe Mazzini, a radical advocate of republicanism, established a new organization, *Giovane Italia* – Young Italy. Unlike the *Carbonari*, who focused upon regional revolution, Mazzini believed in a national state exclusive of foreign powers and monarchies. His movement found support among the educated youth, playing upon romantic notions of revolution in the name of a unified Italy, which would protect individual rights through the creation of a republic.

Mazzini and his supporters raised the banner of revolution between 1831 and 1834. Revolutions extended to the Papal States, Modena, and Piedmont. General Carlo Zucchi, another former Napoleonic general, led volunteers against papal rule. Austrian and French troops were dispatched, defeating Zucchi and his followers. Among the Mazzinians with Zucchi was Louis-Napoleon Bonaparte, nephew of the former French emperor. Louis-Napoleon was captured, but released on papal pardon. The revolutions of 1831 failed. Between 1833 and 1834, Mazzinian plots were foiled in Piedmont,

leading to the arrest and self-imposed exile of many participants. One of the plotters, a sailor in the Piedmontese Navy, Giuseppe Garibaldi, fled to South America in order to escape arrest, and perhaps execution.

The failure of these revolutions led to a mass exodus of liberals wishing to foist constitutions upon their monarchs. In some cases, they desired the abolition of monarchy. Many exiles, like Garibaldi, resettled in the new states of South America, while others traveled to France and then Portugal and Spain, where they found employment as soldiers in the Carlist Wars. The Portuguese and Spanish royal houses were divided between constitutional monarchists and absolutists. These civil wars provided an opportunity for Italian revolutionaries to continue fighting for the cause. By 1848, many who served in the Iberian Peninsula had returned to Italy, prepared to continue the fight when revolution broke out once more.

The First War of Italian Unification, 1848–49

The year 1848 saw revolutions throughout the European continent. In January revolution in Sicily cast off the Neapolitan king. In March 1848 demonstrations in the major cities of the Austrian Empire – Vienna, Prague, Budapest, Cracow, Milan, and Venice – paralyzed the imperial regime. Revolutionaries in Vienna demanded a constitution, while those in the disparate kingdoms and territories of the empire called for greater autonomy. In Hungary and Lombardy–Venetia revolutionaries demanded full independence from the Habsburg crown. In Milan and Venice, the Austrian administration found itself under siege. In the Lombard capital, five days of violence led to the abandonment of the city. Simultaneously, Daniele Manin led the revolution in Venice and ejected the Austrian garrison.

In Tuscany, Naples, Modena, and Parma revolutions forced their monarchs to accept constitutions. In Rome, Pope Pius IX, initially

sympathetic to the revolutions and demands for substantial reform, gave his support but cautioned against violence. Throughout the 1840s the moderate constitutionalists had succeeded in moving their monarchs toward significant political reforms, which had culminated in constitutions by 1848. In Piedmont–Sardinia Charles Albert (who became king in 1831) followed suit, but had promulgated a constitution three years earlier in 1845. His actions sealed his relationship with the reformers although they did not satisfy the Mazzinians. The House of Savoy was seen as progressive, and when revolution came to Lombardy–Venetia, he was pressured to offer immediate material support.

The paralysis of the Austrian government in March 1848 meant that response to the revolutions would be neither swift nor effective. The venerated Habsburg general, Feldmarschall Josef Radetzky, commanded the Austrian army in Lombardy–Venetia. Despite his efforts to contain the violence in Milan and Venice, his army had been reduced in strength in the years preceding 1848 and

The Five Days in Milan of March 18–22, 1848 marked the start of the Italian revolutions. Austrian Feldmarschall Radetzky tried to suppress the Milanese uprising, but the intensity of resistance, and the spread of revolution throughout Austrian Lombardy and Venetia led him to abandon the city and concentrate his army around Verona. The success of the Milanese revolution inspired similar events throughout Austrian Italy and encouraged King Charles Albert of Piedmont–Sardinia to inaugurate the First War of Italian Unification. (De Agostini/Getty Images)

contained no more than 68,000 men. The widespread disturbances in the Austrian Empire, and the rebellion in Hungary, guaranteed that Radetzky would not receive reinforcements in the short term. All of this created an opportunity for Italian nationalists throughout the peninsula, but there remained a clear division between the constitutional monarchists and the republicans.

The Piedmontese parliament, and nationalists such as Camillo di Cavour, Cesare Balbo, and Massimo d'Azeglio encouraged Charles Albert to seize the moment, cross the Lombard frontier with his army, and march on Milan. On March 29,

Radetzky refused to abandon Italy during the revolutions of 1848 despite orders from Vienna in 1848. He fought tenaciously to retain Lombardy–Venetia in the midst of revolution. His military genius led to his victory over Charles Albert at Custozza in 1848 and the rapid defeat of a second Piedmontese campaign at Novara in 1849, shown here. (Mary Evans Picture Library/Imagno)

Charles Albert led his army of 28,000 men across the Ticino River, inaugurating the First War of Italian Unification. The remainder of his army was mobilizing, and would join him over the following weeks. The Piedmontese had numerical parity with Radetzky's forces,

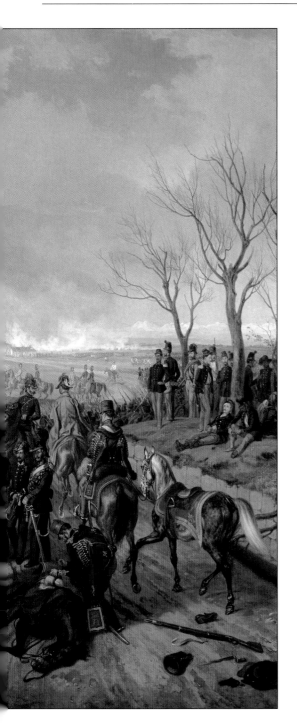

Feldmarschall Josef Radetzky von Radetz commanded the Austrian army in Lombardy–Venetia from the early 1830s through 1857. Radetzky served in Italy as a young officer during Napoleon Bonaparte's Italian campaign of 1796, and became chief of staff to the Army of Bohemia in 1813. He was the most talented and skilled of the 19th-century Habsburg generals (© Ali Meyer/Corbis)

as much of the Austrian Army was dispersed among the cities of Lombardy–Venetia trying to contain the revolutions.

Charles Albert's decision met with widespread support among revolutionaries throughout the peninsula. Indeed, he even garnered support from Pius IX. The Italian monarchs followed suit, not wanting to give the Savoyard king the glory and reputation of "liberating" Italy. Leopold II of Tuscany and Ferdinand II, King of the Two Sicilies, dispatched forces to Lombardy and Venetia. Guglielmo Pepe was given command of the Neapolitan expeditionary corps, while Giovanni Durando, a Piedmontese general and former Mazzinian who had fled in 1830 and fought in Spain, was granted command of the Papal forces. All totaled, the Italian princes intended to commit more than 100,000 men to the north. Princely support, however, was short lived, and combined Italian forces – excluding the Piedmontese Army – never exceeded 20,000 during the war.

The Austrian position in Lombardy–Venetia was precarious. Radetzky withdrew from Milan, and placed Venice under blockade. Austrian commanders in Verona and Mantua threatened the inhabitants, dissuading them from action.

Radetzky, however, understood that in the outlying cities and towns of Austrian-controlled Italy it was impossible to manage everything when facing foreign threats and internal revolution. The Austrian Feldmarschall ordered his generals to withdraw from their distant garrisons and concentrate in the Quadrilateral fortresses of Verona, Mantua, Legnago, and Peschiera. The strong position provided protection for Radetzky's army, and created significant problems for the Piedmontese Army.

Charles Albert entered Milan on March 29 to the cheers of the population. Piedmontese forces advanced to the Mincio, pushing the Austrian rearguard beyond the river. The rapid advance had outpaced reinforcements, and by this time the Papal Army under Durando was south of the Po River, Pepe's Neapolitans had moved further north, and the Tuscan division was en route. The Piedmontese king determined to march on Verona, crossing the Mincio in mid-April. Charles Albert defeated the Austrians at Pastrengo on April 30, and placed Peschiera under siege. Fortified by victory, the Piedmontese advanced upon Verona. Radetzky refused to allow Charles Albert to hold the initiative; he sortied from the city and on May 6 repelled the Piedmontese at Santa Lucia. Charles Albert withdrew to Villafranca, southwest of Verona, and waited for more reinforcements from Piedmont, along with the other Italian armies.

The princes of Parma and Modena succumbed to revolutionary threats and joined their states with Piedmont, which now included Lombardy. Tuscany remained aloof, but committed to the war. The initial support from Pope Pius IX and Ferdinand II waned through April. Pius IX tried to appease the population of Rome, but did not want to commit his forces to war against Austria. He ordered Durando not to advance beyond the Po River. The general argued with the Pontiff, and crossed the river into Venetia, seeking to separate Radetzky from Venice. Papal forces fanned out through Venetia. Guglielmo Pepe's large Neapolitan army never made it across the Po. Despite the granting of a constitution, republican revolutionaries attempted a coup against Ferdinand II. The plot was crushed and the king abrogated the constitution. He then ordered Pepe to return to Naples. The old general refused, but much of his army deserted him. When Pepe finally reached the Po, he had no more than 2,000 men under his command. He joined his paltry forces with the Tuscan division observing Mantua.

Charles Albert failed to coordinate operations with Durando. Radetzky, however, kept in close contact with his generals. A relief column of 16,000 men under Feldmarschall Leutnant Count Nugent arrived in Venetia to stem the advance of the Italian revolutionaries. Radetzky sent them immediately against Durando at Cornuda. Durando withdrew to Vicenza, where he remained surrounded by Austrian forces through June. The relief in Venetia permitted Radetzky to outmaneuver the Piedmontese. While Charles Albert sat at Villafranca, Radetzky's divisions conducted a flank march to Mantua. They defeated the Tuscan and Neapolitan forces at Curtatone–Matanara on May 29 and then, from Mantua, Radetzky moved north along the west bank of the Mincio. The crafty Radetzky threatened to cut Charles Albert and his army off from Piedmont. The movement, however, was discovered and Charles Albert rapidly countermarched to intercept the Austrians. Their armies clashed at Goito on May 30, with the Piedmontese catching the Austrian divisions on the line of march. Defeated, Radetzky withdrew to Mantua. The same day, Peschiera fell.

Charles Albert lacked sufficient forces to besiege Mantua or Verona properly or to continue the offensive into Venetia beyond these victories. The loss of Tuscan, Neapolitan, and Papal military forces removed valuable allies and manpower, though the Piedmontese now mustered 75,000, including thousands of Lombard volunteers. Charles Albert returned to Villafranca and held to his position screening Mantua to the south and Verona to the northeast.

Radetzky received further reinforcements in the early summer, and decided to act. He moved against the Piedmontese from Verona and Mantua. Trapped between two armies Charles Albert fought at Custozza for three days (July 23–25), until his position became untenable. He withdrew across the Mincio to Milan. At this time, the Piedmontese monarch concluded that he had lost the advantage. Radetzky's army appeared before Milan and on August 9 Charles Albert agreed to an armistice. The Piedmontese Army withdrew from Lombardy, ending the war in 1848.

The failure of the Piedmontese campaign spelled disaster for revolutionaries in Lombardy, but did not mark the end of war or revolution in Italy. Venice continued to resist. The revolutionaries in Rome became increasingly disaffected with Pius IX. Moreover, those exiled in the preceding years, including Mazzini and Garibaldi, had returned to Italy by the summer.

Any commander other than Radetzky would have lost his nerve. His determination and stubbornness outlasted the momentary unity of Italian princes and revolutionaries. Nevertheless, the defeat of moderate forces in Naples and northern Italy opened a path for republican revolutions. The Romans rebelled against papal rule in November. Pellegrino Rossi, the papal minister, was murdered on the steps of the Vatican. Pius IX fled to Gaeta, the Neapolitan fortress city across the border. The Italian revolutions entered a new phase.

A Roman republic was declared in February 1849. In Florence a revolution forced Leopold II from the throne. Mazzini led the Triumvirate – an executive comprising three members – in Rome, and his supporters flocked to the city. Giuseppe Garibaldi arrived leading his "Red Shirt" volunteers and was made second in command of the Army of the Republic. These events encouraged Charles Albert and the conservative nationalists. The king believed that, with Austrian forces fighting in Hungary, continued resistance in Venice, and new revolutions in Italy, a second offensive could succeed. This was a fantasy.

In March, one year after his first attempt, Charles Albert assembled an army of 75,000 men on the Lombard frontier. Radetzky did

King Charles Albert of Piedmont–Sardinia (r. 1831–49) led the Piedmontese invasion of Lombardy inaugurating the First War of Italian Unification (1848–49). Defeated at Custozza in 1848 and Novara in 1849, he abdicated the throne to save his kingdom from Austrian occupation. (Interfoto/Sammlung Rauch/Mary Evans)

not wait for the Piedmontese offensive, but struck first. He crossed the Ticino River at Pavia and defeated the Piedmontese at Mortara and then decisively at Novara. Charles Albert lost the battle after two days of fighting. He abdicated the throne in favor of his son to save his kingdom from Austrian occupation. Victor Emmanuel II reluctantly accepted a ten-year truce, and declared void the annexations of Parma and Modena.

Piedmont's crushing defeat was the first in a series of disasters that befell Italian revolutions and national aspirations in 1849. The fate of the papacy rested with the Neapolitans, Austrians, French, and Spanish, the Catholic powers. Ferdinand II marched on Rome twice in the spring, only to have his army defeated by the Romans led by Garibaldi. The Spanish and Austrians prepared relief forces, but it was the new president of France, Louis-Napoleon Bonaparte, who determined to restore Pius IX to the papal throne. He dispatched General

Charles Oudinot with 10,000 men to retake the city. Once again, Garibaldi succeeded in repelling a foreign army. Two months later, Oudinot returned with 30,000 men and a siege corps. Garibaldi and the Roman army suffered a month of bombardment before the French guns breached the walls and compelled the republic to surrender.

Garibaldi and the remnants of his volunteers fled Rome to avoid capture. He led his forces through the Apennines in an attempt to reach Daniele Manin and Venice. Pursued doggedly by the Spanish and the Austrians, Garibaldi's "Red Shirts" were worn down. At San Marino, Garibaldi ordered the army to disperse and escape as best as they could. Narrowly avoiding capture, Garibaldi made his way to the Tuscan coast where he took to the sea and exile once again. Manin,

too, went into exile shortly thereafter as Venice surrendered.

The Italian revolutions of 1848–49 ended in disaster for both the liberal moderates and the Mazzinian republicans. Charles Albert had abdicated and Mazzini, Garibaldi, and Manin were in exile. Far from ending desires for constitutions and national unity, the defeat ushered in a decade of reconstruction and planning. Victor Emmanuel II, the new king of Piedmont–Sardinia, appointed Massimo d'Azeglio prime minister and Camillo di Cavour minister of finance. Revolutionaries flocked to Piedmont, the only remaining constitutional state in Italy. The Piedmontese Army incorporated many former revolutionaries who had returned from exile.

The Italian Kingdoms, France, and Austria

The decade following the revolutions and suppression of 1848–49 saw the introduction of neo-absolutism in Austria, the preservation of conservatism in Naples, and the end of reforms in the Papal States. Mazzinian principles of republicanism had failed. Nationalists turned to Piedmont–Sardinia and Victor Emmanuel II, who preserved his father's constitution, but acted against republicanism. It appeared as if national aspirations had suffered their final blow.

The Kingdom of Piedmont–Sardinia

The debacle of 1848–49 led to sweeping changes in Piedmont. Victor Emmanuel II determined to succeed where his father had failed. His association with the moderates

and nationalists guaranteed the security of his throne from revolution. Indeed, the House of Savoy remained conscious of the internal threat from the Army after the events of 1821. The minister of war and the chief of staff of the Piedmontese Army were consistently drawn from men who had never participated in the revolutions of 1821 or the early 1830s. Victor Emmanuel did not depart from that royal policy, and played upon the notion that the Savoyard throne was

The Piedmontese Army was reorganized following the defeat of 1848–49, and by the time of the war of 1859–61 was a modern, effective army. Here, the 4th Division of the Piedmontese Army under General Enrico Cialdini crosses the Sesia at Vercelli before attacking the Austrian battalions at the battle of Palestro. The success of the 4th Division marked the first offensive action against the Austrian Army. (Anne S.K. Brown Military Collection, Brown University Library)

progressive and supportive of the liberation of Italy. He recruited to his banner Giovanni Durando, Enrico Cialdini, and Manfredo Fanti. All had been committed revolutionaries in their youth, had fled between 1831 and 1834, and had served in Portugal and Spain, only to return to Italy in 1848. Their credentials as moderates and nationalists combined with their military experience made them perfect officers for Victor Emmanuel's army. His regime represented some of the most prominent constitutionalists and nationalists. Nevertheless, the king and his administration remained wary of Mazzinians.

The most significant appointment to Victor Emmanuel's administration came in

Alessandro La Marmora, brother of Alfonso La Marmora, established the Bersaglieri corps in 1836. The Bersaglieri were elite light infantry who were trained to advance on the double and run. They were often employed for reconnaissance and advanced-guard duty. These highly trained troops were equipped with rifled carbines, which were devastating to the Papal troops at Castelfidardo. (Anne S.K. Brown Military Collection, Brown University Library)

1849, when Camillo di Cavour became minister of finance. In 1852, he succeeded D'Azeglio as prime minister, but Cavour kept the finance portfolio. Cavour understood the critical importance of economic development. He believed that industrialization, railroad construction, and the financial independence of the kingdom from British banks would provide the king with the tools necessary to challenge Austria in the future. Under Cavour, Piedmont ended its long financial relationship with Great Britain, and entered into agreements with French banks and investors. There were a number of prominent Italian bankers, such as Alexander Bixio, who had established their connections in Paris prior to 1848. France appeared as a better ally than Britain with the election of Louis-Napoleon to the Presidency of the French Republic, and his subsequent elevation to Emperor of the French as Napoleon III in 1852.

Cavour presided over an impressive building program, which increased industrial production, exponentially expanded rail lines, and encouraged trade. Piedmont became a prosperous state during the 1850s. Cavour built his relationship with France, while maintaining friendship with Great Britain. He sought opportunities to ingratiate the kingdom with the larger powers. It was clear to all, including Victor Emmanuel, that any attempt to chase Austria from Lombardy–Venetia would require a foreign military alliance. Napoleon III seemed the most likely candidate. His uncle, the great conqueror Napoleon I, had established his reputation in 1796–97 by defeating the Austrians in Italy.

The experience of 1848–49 led to extensive military reforms and strategic planning. General Alfonso La Marmora reorganized the Piedmontese Army, its conscription system, and the division between the active and reserve army. Further railroad construction permitted the development of an improved mobilization system: a problem that had plagued Charles Albert in 1848. The introduction of telegraph lines, established along with the expanded rail network, allowed for better communication within the kingdom. All of this had military applications.

The outbreak of the Crimean War in 1854 provided Cavour with an opportunity to become actively allied to France and Great Britain in their war against Russia. The conflict would also permit the newly refurbished Piedmontese Army to acquire further experience on the battlefield. In May 1855, an expeditionary corps of 18,000 men landed in the Crimea. Under La Marmora and Durando, the Piedmontese fought alongside the French and British at the Cernaya and Malakoff. At the Congress of Paris in 1856, Cavour had an invitation to sit at the peace table as an equal. This was a major step toward his goal of removing Austria from Italy.

When war came in 1859, the Piedmontese Army was well led, well motivated and highly trained. The Army possessed an excellent staff corps, and the experiences of 1848–49 and 1855 provided valuable lessons for future military operations. The Piedmontese Army was equipped with percussion-cap muskets, Model 1844, but the elite Bersaglieri (light infantry) battalions possessed the Model 1856 rifled carbine, which used the Minié ball. It was a modern army in all ways, although the Piedmontese Army still employed smoothbore artillery.

France

Louis-Napoleon Bonaparte had a special affinity for Italy. The entire Bonaparte clan had settled there after his uncle's defeat and exile in 1814. Louis-Napoleon became an ardent supporter of constitutionalism, and this led to his participation in the Mazzinian revolution of 1834. His pardon by Pope Gregory XVI saved his life, and perhaps made him sympathetic to the papacy on a personal level, but his political aspirations in 1848 made his support from Catholics a necessity. The dispatch of French forces to Rome in 1849 was meant to shore up his support from French Catholics, and prevent the Austrians or Spanish from saving the Pontiff and gaining the glory.

Napoleon III, Emperor of the French (r. 1852–70) presided over the Second French Empire. He was the nephew of Napoleon I, the son of Napoleon's brother Louis. Prior to his election as President of the Second French Republic in 1849, Louis-Napoleon was a member of Young Italy, and an anti-clerical. He was the pretender to the Bonapartist throne, staging a *coup d'état* in 1851, overthrowing the Second Republic. Napoleon III committed France to war with Austria in 1859.
© Michael Nicholson/Corbis)

Louis-Napoleon's ambitions did not end with his election as President of the Second Republic in December 1848. He continued to curry favor with conservatives and the military leadership, which enabled him to effect a *coup d'état* in 1851. A year later, on the anniversary of his uncle's coronation as emperor, December 2, Louis-Napoleon took the crown as Napoleon III. The establishment of the Second French Empire was followed by the desire to export French power without disturbing the diplomatic balance in Europe.

The Crimean War provided this opportunity. France sided with Great Britain and the Ottoman Empire, to contain Russian objectives of dominating the Balkans and controlling the Black Sea. A French army in excess of 120,000 men provided the largest military contingent. Victory over Russia allowed Napoleon III to claim that his uncle's defeat in 1812 had been avenged.

Cavour understood this quite well, and during the Paris conference sought to play on Bonapartist desires to come to grips with the Austrians too. Cavour employed his beautiful niece, the Countess of Castiglione, to gain the emperor's favor through a liaison. It did not take a great deal of effort to press Napoleon III to publicly support Italian aspirations. Throughout 1856 and 1857, Napoleon spoke frequently of the Italian situation. By 1858, however, his public interest in Italy had waned.

The French Imperial Army he commanded was one of the most technologically advanced

Rifled muskets and artillery increased the accuracy, range, and lethality of weapons. Casualties at the battle of Magenta, pictured here, were quite high at nearly 15,000 killed and wounded, reflecting the changing nature of military technology. At Solferino the numbers were even higher, with nearly 40,000 total casualties. (The Art Archive/Palazzo Pitti Florence/Collection Dagli Orti)

Austria

The Habsburg dynasty came close to collapse in 1848. At the height of revolution the court ordered Radetzky to abandon Lombardy–Venetia. He refused and by late spring members of the court had found refuge in Verona, one of the safest cities in the empire. Among them was 18-year-old Franz Josef, the nephew of Emperor Ferdinand I and heir to the throne. The scion of the House of Austria stood with Radetzky at Santa Lucia and Custozza. Joining the noble entourage was Prince Felix zu Schwarzenberg, a disciple of Metternich and a general. In October 1848 the Austrian Army reclaimed Vienna and Franz Josef became emperor with Schwarzenberg as his prime minister.

Under Schwarzenberg's guidance and with the support of the generals, Franz Josef pursued a neo-absolutist agenda. The young emperor accepted a constitution, but revised it upon his terms. He redeemed his empire with bayonets and gunpowder. The Army stood tall under the new emperor. The Austrian administration in Lombardy–Venetia remained under Radetzky's control through 1857. During this time Franz Josef's military advisor, Feldmarschall Leutnant Karl Ludwig Count Grünne, reduced the influence of the old generals and introduced more pliable acolytes. Radetzky despised Grünne, and his obstinacy became apparent during the Crimean War, when Austria retained its neutrality but mobilized. Radetzky refused to permit regiments from his army in Italy to be transferred to commands in the east. After the war Grünne facilitated Radetzky's retirement in 1857. Feldzeugmeister Franz Count Gyulai, one of Grünne's close friends, assumed command of the Austrian 2nd Army in Italy.

in the world. The soldiers were uniformly equipped with a percussion-cap rifled musket that used the Minié ball, invented by French captain Claude Minié. In 1858, the Army introduced the Lahitte rifled artillery system. By April 1859, all artillery batteries with the army in Italy possessed these guns. Although their rate of fire was not significantly greater than the traditional smoothbore, range and accuracy were much improved. They would play a pivotal role during the war in Italy.

The French Army introduced the Lahitte system in 1858. The strength of French industry enabled sufficient production of the new rifled artillery to properly equip all the batteries sent to Italy in 1859. Neither the Piedmontese nor the Austrians possessed rifled artillery. It played a critical role at Solferino. (PHGCOM)

Grünne's military administration created friction in Vienna and in the regional army headquarters. Financial crisis further reduced the ability of the war ministry to maintain the Army at existing levels. When Gyulai took post in Milan, the 2nd Army had shrunk from more than 100,000 men to fewer than 60,000. The reduction in forces made matters worse, as the 2nd Army was responsible for maintaining a garrison in the Papal States at Bologna. It was an agreement made in 1849 upon the restoration of Pius IX to the temporal throne.

By 1858, Austria held firm in Lombardy–Venetia but it no longer possessed military dominance in the region. Any future conflict in northern Italy would require reinforcement from the various armies deployed in Galicia, Bohemia, and Austria. The mobilization and movement of forces throughout the empire was less of a problem in 1858 than a decade earlier. As in Piedmont, Lombardy–Venetia had seen the expansion of railroads, linking Milan with Venice and the empire's interior. Milan was equally tied across the Ticino River to Piedmont.

The Imperial–Royal Army managed to maintain technological parity with its rivals.

Although financial difficulties and limited industry prevented the production of rifled artillery, the infantry was equipped with the solid Lorenz rifle. Like the Minié rifle, the Lorenz had good range and accuracy. When the 2nd Army marched to war in 1859, its soldiers did not suffer any qualitative disadvantage in weaponry in the field, except in artillery.

The Kingdom of the Two Sicilies

The Kingdom of the Two Sicilies (Naples) possessed the second-largest army in the Italian peninsula, and the third-largest navy in the Mediterranean after those of France and Spain. The Neapolitan Navy surpassed that of Piedmont–Sardinia and that of the Austrian Empire. Its geographical position required substantial sea power to protect its coastlines and the island of Sicily. Nevertheless, the Neapolitan Navy failed to prevent Garibaldi and his volunteers from landing in Sicily in May 1860, and then again on the mainland in September. The Army therefore remained the prop and support of the monarchy. Revolutions in 1799, 1821, and 1848, however, meant that the kings of Naples could not rely solely on conscripted rank and file to preserve the throne, but employed professionals and hired foreign regiments.

Sicily had always been difficult to rule. The island had revolted despite the granting of the initial constitution and required a formal military expedition in September 1848 to restore monarchical control. Throughout the 1850s local unrest continued, and in 1857 Carlo Piscane led a short-lived rebellion to liberate the island. Revolution in Sicily was the product of liberal constitutionalism, which had its greatest support in Palermo, the commercial center of the island, and the desire of the peasantry to challenge any central authority. One-third of the Neapolitan Army was deployed therefore in Palermo, Siracusa, and Messina to quell potential revolutions.

In 1860, King Francis II commanded an army of 95,000 men, which served to protect the monarchy from its own population rather than the Papal frontier to the north. Although the minister of war, General Filangieri, and senior generals such as Paolo Ruffo di Castelcicala and General Lanza were drawn from loyal Neapolitan professionals, Francis employed foreign officers, such as the Swiss Colonel von Mechel, to command foreign regiments. Foreign infantry regiments and several light infantry – Cacciatori – battalions were recruited in Switzerland, Bavaria, and Austria and deployed as part of the garrison in Sicily. The threat of revolution was never far from the Neapolitan king; his harsh policies led to popular disaffection and were one of the central reasons for the rapid collapse of his regime in 1860.

Austrian troops – shown here in a cemetery – took advantage of every aspect of terrain and buildings to impede the advance of French troops at Magenta on June 4. (Anne S.K. Brown Military Collection, Brown University Library)

Toward conflict

The 1850s was a period of substantial economic growth in northern Italy. Cavour and his colleagues in the National Society, an organization established in 1857 to support the movement for national unification, benefited from this nascent commercial reality. They believed that economic unification would precede political unification, but that did not stop Cavour from seeking an opportunity to force the issue. The years between the Congress of Paris (1856) and 1858 provided enormous diplomatic opportunities to garner support from France, Great Britain, and Russia. The Austrian government was firmly entrenched in Vienna, but its inaction during the Crimean War and Franz Josef's interest in reinforcing Habsburg power in the German Confederation alienated Russia and Prussia. As Austria gradually faced diplomatic isolation, Cavour determined to seal an agreement with Napoleon III.

Revolutions, plots, and planning

Cavour understood that war with Austria required support from France and the National Society, but he feared republican revolution. He maintained close ties with Giuseppe La Farina, a leader of the National Society, and encouraged continued association with its members in Tuscany, Parma, and Modena. Mazzinian plots, however, became commonplace in 1857 in Sicily, Piedmont, and France. Although Cavour cared little for the Bourbons of Naples, the intrigue in Piedmont threatened the constitutional monarchy, and in Paris Mazzinian assassins were arrested as they conducted surveillance on the apartment of Cavour's niece and Napoleon III's mistress, the Countess of Castiglione. In January 1858 Felice Orsini, a former disciple of Mazzini, and three compatriots threw bombs at Napoleon III and his entourage as they arrived at the Paris Opera. The French emperor escaped the attempt on his life, and the assassins were caught. Cavour feared that the Orsini bomb plot would end any hope of a French alliance. Subsequent events proved otherwise.

Orsini's trial altered Napoleon III's perception of the Italian question. Orsini argued that Napoleon III had betrayed Italian patriots by his lack of action. The French emperor was shocked that he was viewed in this manner. He was sympathetic to the Italian cause, but did not consider it an immediate priority. Orsini was executed in March, but his appeal to Napoleon III during the trial compelled the emperor to reassess his Italian policy. Over the next several months Napoleon III and Cavour communicated through intermediaries. They met in secret on July 21, 1858, at Plombières.

The meeting at Plombières created enormous opportunity for Cavour. The trial and the public debate concerning France and its relationship with the Italian question

deeply concerned Vienna. Cavour encouraged this agitation, as it raised tensions. After a day of discussion Napoleon III and Cavour made a verbal agreement that set the course for Piedmont–Sardinia and Italian nationalists. The arrangement centered on a defensive alliance between the two states. If Austria attacked Piedmont, France would come to its aid and make common cause until Lombardy and Venetia were free of the Habsburgs. The price for victory was the patrimonial lands of Victor Emmanuel II and the kings of Piedmont–Sardinia, the predominantly French-speaking Duchy of Savoy and County of Nice. The French emperor requested that the alliance be sealed by the marriage of his cousin Prince Jérôme Napoleon to Princess Clothilde, daughter of King Victor Emmanuel II. Cavour agreed to the principles. He and Napoleon III discussed the shape of Italy after the war. A northern Italian kingdom under the House of Savoy would include Lombardy, Venetia, Modena, and Parma. A kingdom in central Italy would be formed from Tuscany and the Romagna and Papal Legations. The Kingdom of the Two Sicilies would remain independent in the south.

Over the next five months Cavour prepared for the coming conflict. The prevailing diplomatic system in Europe demanded that France intervene only in defense of its ally. Cavour, then, had to goad Austria into war. He encouraged the activities of the National Society in Lombardy and recruited Garibaldi. The Piedmontese prime minister determined to use Garibaldi to lead a revolution in Tuscany and the duchies, diverting Austrian forces from Lombardy. The representatives of Napoleon III and Cavour met in Paris in December to sign the first of two conventions codifying the verbal agreements made at Plombières, and establishing articles concerning the joint military effort.

The city of Alessandria was strategically placed at the confluence of the Po and Sesia rivers. Its fortifications defended the vital crossroads and rail lines running from Genoa to Turin. (Anne S.K. Brown Military Collection, Brown University Library)

On New Year's Eve 1859, Napoleon III spoke with Baron Hübner, Austria's ambassador to France. The emperor relayed his dismay that relations between the two empires had deteriorated. This message signaled Napoleon III's plans to pave the diplomatic path to war. Less than three weeks later Prince Jérôme Napoleon and General Adolphe Niel arrived in Turin. The formalities of the marriage contract required a formal proposal and then the wedding. All of this provided proper cover for clandestine planning. While the prince played courtier, General Niel spent the next two weeks meeting with Alfonso La Marmora, minister of war, and the senior generals of the Piedmontese Army. Strategy discussions in the capital were followed by several days of touring the Lombard frontier and surveying the fortifications of Casale and Alessandria

Cavour received regular reports from La Marmora, preferring to keep his distance. He invited Garibaldi to Turin. His legendary appeal to Italian revolutionaries after the defense of Rome in 1849 would enable Cavour to draw revolutionaries to his side, and perhaps temper Mazzinian animosity toward the Piedmontese throne. Garibaldi had grown distant from Mazzini during his time in Rome and the years that followed.

He arrived in Turin at the end of January 1859 and met with Cavour. The prime minister had increased tensions with Austria by encouraging Lombards and Venetians to avoid military service by fleeing to Piedmont. Garibaldi would train and lead the volunteers if he declared his support for Victor Emmanuel. A Garibaldinian army in the duchies would divert Austrian forces from Lombardy. Subsequently the volunteer campaign was too successful, and in less than four weeks, at the end of February, Cavour had to order the program halted as thousands crossed the frontier and events moved too quickly. When war came at the end of April, almost 20,000 Italians had arrived in Piedmont, ready to fight.

The lessons of 1848 were not lost on Cavour, Victor Emmanuel, La Marmora, and the senior officers of the Piedmontese Army. In January La Marmora redeployed the army to the east, and in February he recalled men from leave. During the first week of March Victor Emmanuel decreed mobilization.

The Piedmontese railroads expanded exponentially during the decade of the 1850s. Cavour and his government saw industrial development as a means to increase Piedmont's wealth and status in Italy. He did not realize that the railroads would play a central role in strategy and operations during the Second War of Italian Unification. (Alinari Archives, Florence via Getty Images)

All of this ensured that when war came, the Army would be at full strength. In January the Army had 35,947 men under arms; by the end of April 77,348 men filled the ranks. To be sure, the secret military agreement between France and Piedmont placed on Turin the responsibility of financing the French war effort and supply. Several months were required to make proper logistical arrangements. Extended military preparations had a second purpose – to agitate Vienna.

The Austrians kept close watch on events in Italy. Baron Hübner's report to Franz Josef after the New Year raised concerns that war with France loomed. Nevertheless, the immediate issue became Cavour's machinations in Lombardy and the gradual mobilization of the Piedmontese Army. Count Grünne and Feldmarschall Heinrich Baron Hess, the Chief of Staff of the Imperial–Royal Army, determined to reinforce Gyulai's 2nd Army in February. Austria, however, suffered from a weak economy and wartime mobilization was to be avoided if at all possible. Soldiers on leave and those on reserve were recalled to their regiments in Italy, but this was insufficient in case of war. Gyulai's army mustered merely 44,837 men in January. The regiments were dispersed in garrisons throughout Lombardy and Venetia. Hess ordered three additional corps to Lombardy, which arrived respectively in March and April. When war came the 2nd Army marshaled 110,235 men and an additional 59,000 deployed in the towns and cities of Lombardy–Venetia, to maintain order. Throughout, Vienna issued several threats to Turin, demanding immediate demobilization or war. This played into the hands of Cavour and Napoleon III.

Although history has portrayed Napoleon III as a failed shadow of his uncle, the French emperor consistently demonstrated a keen diplomatic sense during the first decade of his reign. His insistence that Austria strike first insulated France from accusations of aggression. As war loomed in early 1859 the

British acted to defuse the crisis, seeking an international congress to settle the issue. Napoleon III agreed to such a meeting, as he could not refuse and still remain the "protector" of a smaller state. He simultaneously conducted secret negotiations with the Russians, without the knowledge of his foreign minister Count Walewski.

Czar Alexander II blamed Franz Josef for Russia's defeat in the Crimea. The Russians had saved Franz Josef's empire in 1849–50 by dispatching an army to assist in suppressing the Hungarian revolt. When in 1854 war came, the Russians demanded that Austria come to their aid. Franz Josef wisely decided to remain neutral, though he played both sides. In 1859, Czar Alexander saw his opportunity to repay the favor. In March France and Russia concluded a secret agreement that guaranteed Russian neutrality if war broke out between Austria and France. Napoleon III kept this from Cavour.

The French emperor revealed his true intentions to only a few of his senior officers. General Niel was integrally involved in planning, as were General Émile Fleury and Marshal Victor de Castellane. Niel

Napoleon III's Imperial Guard Corps fought at both Magenta and Solferino. At Magenta, the Guard Chasseur regiments supported MacMahon's attack on Magenta while the Zouaves fought their way across the Ponte Nuovo and crossed the Naviglio Grande by boat. Their actions were critical to the French victory. (Anne S.K. Brown Military Collection, Brown University Library)

coordinated the movement of French corps to Italy with the Piedmontese general staff. Fleury was responsible for logistical planning, and Castellane commanded the Armée de Lyon, a large part of the French Army destined for Italy. From February through April French divisions from the Armée d'Afrique in Algeria were redeployed to France. The Atlantic Fleet reinforced the French Mediterranean fleet, in preparation for war. The gradual build-up of French forces at Lyon, Marseilles, and Toulon paralleled the rising tensions between Austria, France and Piedmont. By the third week of April more than 120,000 men were prepared to move to Italy by land and sea. This military concentration was not followed by substantial logistical preparation in France, leading Austrian observers to believe that the French Army was incapable of immediate operations. This was purposely misleading, and enabled Napoleon III to appear measured in his response to Austria, and willing to negotiate.

In April Lord Malmesbury, the British foreign minister, succeeded in arranging a congress on the Italian question. Napoleon III accepted the invitation, as did the Russians and Prussians. Franz Josef agreed to it, as he and his advisors were divided on war. Cavour fell into depression, believing that his years of work and months of planning would come to naught. A congress would permit tensions to dissipate, and it seemed that Napoleon III was going to abandon his agreements. This was far from the truth. The French emperor agreed to the congress, but never departed from military planning. In any event, it was the Austrians who acted precipitously. On April 23 the Austrian ambassador to Turin presented King Victor Emmanuel II with an ultimatum. If the Piedmontese did not withdraw from the frontier of Lombardy and demobilize their army, Austria would go to war. Victor Emmanuel had three days to respond.

The imperial court was divided over the issue of war. Franz Josef made the decision based upon the belief that in case of war, the German Confederation would mobilize against France. This was a false assumption. Perhaps most important was the concern that the diplomatic climate in Europe did not favor Austria. Franz Josef feared that while a congress would reduce the threat of war, it would not guarantee the integrity of his kingdom of Lombardy–Venetia. Under these circumstances he issued the demands. Cavour immediately forwarded the ultimatum by telegram to Paris. It arrived at 5pm. Napoleon III responded, ordering his armed forces to move from their staging areas to Piedmont.

Austrian Hussars of the Hesse-Cassel regiment in bivouac, c.1859. The Austrian cavalry in Italy were in equal number to their French counterparts, but were not properly employed for reconnaissance. (Anne S.K. Brown Military Collection, Brown University Library)

The Second War of Italian Unification, 1859–61

The war against Austria, April–July 1859

The war in 1859 can be divided into three phases: the defensive phase, April 24–May 12; the offensive phase, May 12–June 24; and the Armistice of Villafranca, June 25–July 11, 1859. During the first phase, Cavour's and Napoleon III's intrigues reached their culmination, but the Piedmontese Army had to hold out long enough for the French to arrive in theater. The successful redeployment of the French army in Italy was followed by the arrival of Napoleon III in Piedmont, and the joint Franco-Piedmontese offensive. After five weeks of hard fighting, at Montebello, Palestro, Magenta, and Solferino, the Austrians offered terms. Despite prewar

A view of the railroad over the Adda at Cassano. The strategic use of the railroad enabled the rapid deployment of the French Army to Italy, its operational shift to Vercelli, and its subsequent ability to provide logistical support for the allied armies across Lombardy. Piedmontese rail allowed pontoon and bridging equipment to be brought rapidly to the front. Instead of waiting for days before wagons could bring the pontoons, trains brought them in a matter of hours. (M. Mandelli and F. Testa, *Cassano d'Adda e il 1859*, private collection)

planning on all sides, the war did not develop entirely as expected.

Feldzeugmeister Gyulai viewed the coming war with great trepidation. He was a solid administrator, but not a field commander. In the previous months, he had begged for Grünne to replace him. Instead, Feldmarschall Hess dispatched Colonel Franz Kuhn von Kuhnenfeld, an outstanding staff officer, to Milan to assist the commander of the 2nd Army. Gyulai despised Kuhn and refused to speak with him in the weeks preceding the war.

When the Austrian ultimatum was finally issued to Piedmont, Gyulai and his staff determined that they would have a week or two to defeat the Piedmontese prior to the arrival of the French army. All agreed that the quickest way to victory was a direct movement on Turin, following the rail line from Milan. This axis of advance would provide the 2nd Army with proper logistical support from Lombardy, and perhaps compel Victor Emmanuel to negotiate rather than lose his capital.

The Franco-Piedmontese staffs meticulously planned the movement of French forces to Italy via sea and rail. The French railroads were

sufficiently large to rapidly move the Imperial Guard Corps from Paris and two corps from Lyon to the ports of Marseilles and Toulon, whence the French Mediterranean fleet would transport them to Genoa. Two additional corps would travel by rail into Savoy, march through the Alpine passes, and then board Piedmontese trains for Turin.

Trains were reserved, timetables calculated, and supplies prepared for the French army. Franco-Piedmontese planners estimated that it would take ten days to move the entire French campaign army to Italy in this manner. Piedmont possessed rail capacity to move 53,566 men; horses, wagons and artillery would reduce that amount, but it was sufficient. Travel from Turin to Alessandria, the rail hub on the Sesia River, was less than six hours, and it took no more than three from Genoa to Alessandria. Rail capacity also permitted the Piedmontese to supply French forces at the railheads at Susa, after they crossed the Alps, and in Genoa. Magazines at Susa, Genoa, Alessandria, and Turin held supplies for an army of 340,000 men for four days. The Franco-Piedmontese army never exceeded 200,000 combined, and therefore was amply supplied. Charles Poplimont, a Belgian journalist traveling with French forces, commented in his diary on the enormous quantities of food and other military essentials when he arrived at Genoa in the first days of May.

Confidence in the deployment plan did not remove the fear that if the Austrian 2nd Army advanced upon Turin, the Piedmontese would be hard pressed to stop them. Lieutenant Colonel Giuseppe Govone, chief of military intelligence, kept close watch on the positions of the Austrian corps. He possessed an extensive network of spies who relayed vital information on the Austrian forces. Until the end of April, the 2nd Army was dispersed along the Ticino River, the border between Lombardy and Piedmont. La Marmora and the senior generals had decided much earlier to abandon a forward defense of the Lomellina, the region between the Sesia and Ticino.

It was there that in 1849 Radetzky had defeated Charles Albert at Novara by a rapid advance.

The Piedmontese positioned four of their five divisions between Casale, Alessandria, and Novi, to protect the central route to Turin, and the road and rail lines from Genoa. The Piedmontese left one cavalry and one infantry division along the Dora Baltea river blocking the direct route from Turin to Milan. An Austrian advance would be delayed by cavalry, and then held on the Dora Baltea, east of the capital. Two French corps (III and IV), were expected in Turin and would reinforce the Dora Baltea line to pin Gyulai's army, while the remaining three corps (I, II, and the Imperial Guard) moved from Genoa to Alessandria, threatening the 2nd Army's flank.

Victor Emmanuel and his army prepared for the invasion after the reception of the Austrian ultimatum. In Paris, Napoleon III authorized operations. The organization of the armies was as follows:

The French Armée d'Italie:

Imperial Guard Corps	General Reynaud de Saint-Angély
I Corps	Marshal Louis-Achille Baraguey d'Hilliers
II Corps	General Patrice de MacMahon
III Corps	Marshal François Certain Canrobert
IV Corps	General Adolphe Niel
V Corps (forming)	Prince Jérôme Napoleon

The Piedmontese Army:

1st Division	General Angelo Bongiovanni, Prince of Castelborgo
2nd Division	General Manfredo Fanti
3rd Division	General Giovanni Durando
4th Division	General Enrico Cialdini
5th Division	General Domenico Cucchiari
Cavalry Division	General Calisto Bertone di Sambuy

The Austrian 2nd Army:

II Korps	Feldmarschall Leutnant Eduard Prince von Liechtenstein
III Korps	Feldmarschall Leutnant Edmund Prince von Schwarzenberg
V Korps	Feldmarschall Leutnant Count Rudolph Philipp Stadion
VII Korps	Feldmarschall Leutnant Johann Baron Zobel
VIII Korps	Feldmarschall Leutnant Ludwig August Ritter von Benedek
IX Korps	Feldmarschall Leutnant Karl Urban

Austrian Jäger (light infantry) were identifiable on the battlefield by their distinctive gray uniforms. (Anne S.K. Brown Military Collection, Brown University Library)

The French and Piedmontese navies prepared to transport 70,000 men to Genoa in a matter of days. Coordination of operations was conducted via telegraph, and through an exchange of officers. Piedmontese naval captain Pompeo Provana del Sabbione departed for Toulon on March 9, while his French counterpart, a Captain Chaigneau, arrived in Genoa incognito on April 18. Admiral Charles Jacquinot, the maritime prefect at Toulon, and Count Giuseppe Carlo de Rey, captain of the port of Genoa, synchronized the enormous naval operations.

There was little concern about the Austrian Navy. Its strength was comparable to that of the Piedmontese, but France had the second-largest navy in the world, after Great Britain. Archduke Ferdinand Maximilian, commander of the Austrian fleet, prepared to defend the coastline in the Adriatic, but never considered offensive operations. During the first days of the war the Franco-Piedmontese fleets carried out transport in squadrons. Within a few days, however, the ships operated independently to speed deployment.

Speed had been the critical element in Austrian strategy too. Yet, while Vienna waited for the response to the ultimatum, French and Piedmontese forces moved. When on April 26 Victor Emmanuel rejected Franz Josef's demands, 10,000 French troops disembarked in Genoa. Even after the ultimatum was refused the Austrians did not move for the next three days. The reasons for the delay remain unclear. After the war Gyulai claimed that Vienna had ordered him to wait before crossing the Ticino, but at court they placed the blame on the commander of the 2nd Army. It is certain, however, that Franz Josef, Grünne, and Hess believed that a diplomatic arrangement was possible despite the ultimatum. Moreover, they anticipated declarations in Prussia and the German Confederation against French intervention. It was only on April 29 that an Austrian advanced guard crossed the border and began a lethargic advance into the Lomellina. On that day Marshal Baraguey d'Hilliers' I Corps boarded trains in Genoa, heading north to Novi, and the first division of Marshal Canrobert's III Corps descended

the Alpine pass to Susa. By May 1 the immediate crisis had passed and La Marmora confidently wrote to Durando, commanding the 3rd Division at Novi, that the Austrian advance was "*molto lentamente*" – very slow.

A small contingent of Austrian troops crossed the Sesia River at Vercelli but did not move aggressively toward the Dora Baltea and Turin. Intelligence reports from Vienna arrived regularly at Gyulai's headquarters and confirmed the movement of the French army. This information contributed to Gyulai's timid offensive. His staff overestimated the number of French troops in theater, and Gyulai spent another several days deciding whether to push his corps beyond the Sesia. The 2nd Army spent the first week of May dispersed throughout the Lomellina, with only a brigade from VII Korps at Vercelli, and II, III, and V Korps deployed between Casale and Alessandria. Not until ten days after the rejection of the ultimatum did the Austrian army slide to the northwest toward Vercelli.

The advance of the Austrian army in force posed a threat to the weakened position on the Dora Baltea. Victor Emmanuel initially insisted on keeping with the original plan of reinforcing the river line with the French IV Corps, but Marshal Canrobert convinced the king that repositioning the Piedmontese and French forces at Alessandria would offer better strategic opportunities. Gyulai's management

Piedmontese cavalry regiments were attached to French corps during the first weeks of the war. At Montebello Piedmontese cavalry squadrons engaged Austrian troops advancing from the north, preventing them from attacking Forey's divisions. (Anne S.K. Brown Military Collection, Brown University Library)

of the invasion thus far had proved Canrobert right, but by May 7–8 the Austrians could easily push aside the Piedmontese cavalry left on the Dora Baltea if they desired.

On the day that the three Austrian corps crossed the Sesia, the French had more than 110,000 men in Italy.

Arrival of French troops at Genoa

Date	Troops per day	Total arrived
Apr 26	9,920	9,920
Apr 27	1,436	11,356
Apr 28	6,636	17,992
Apr 29	12,783	30,775
Apr 30	9,177	39,952
May 1	10,170	50,122
May 2	7,624	57,746
May 3	1,256	59,002
May 4	224	59,226
May 5	162	59,388
May 6	850	60,238
May 7	670	60,908
May 8	3,205	64,113
May 9	2,281	66,394
May 10	3,067	69,461
May 11	2,917	72,378
May 12	1,220	73,598

Marshal Canrobert's III Corps and General Niel's IV Corps marched through the Alps into Piedmont. They arrived at the railhead at Susa and were transported to Turin. (Anne S.K. Brown Military Collection, Brown University Library)

The threat to Turin abated more quickly than it materialized. The staff of the 2nd Army found it troubling that the Piedmontese and French armies remained in position between Casale and Novi. Discussion ensued that the French marshals were planning a *manoeuvre sur la derrière*, a flank march south of the Po River and into Lombardy, as Napoleon Bonaparte had achieved in 1796. Gyulai responded by withdrawing his corps toward Mortara. Gablenz's brigade remained at Vercelli, and VIII Korps held its position to the south, along the Po. This movement was completed by May 12, the same day that Napoleon III arrived in Genoa on his flagship *Reine Hortense*.

The ghost of Napoleon was ever present during this war. Throughout the planning stage and during the course of the campaign Piedmontese, Austrian, and French generals were constantly reminded of the campaigns fought in 1796 and 1800. They stood on the same battlefields; looking to the past was more than an academic exercise. The day after the Austrian ultimatum Napoleon III asked the advice of Baron Antoine-Henri Jomini, the long-retired and admired military theorist and former Napoleonic general. Jomini's response was that once the French and Piedmontese armies had joined there were several options for an offensive:

Once the union is effected, it must be decided if they will move on the right toward Piacenza, or the center on Pavia, or the left on Magenta. In order to maneuver on the right, they must cross the Po, flanked by the Austrians, facing a considerable army between two fortified camps, and risk, in case of being checked, thrown back upon Genoa … To attack Pavia in the center is taking the "bull by the horns" and risking a reverse without great results in case of success. It is then evident that there is nothing better than to go back to Charles Albert's plan of 1849, and pass the Ticino on the extreme right of the Austrians. But it is indispensible to cover the route from Pavia to Vercelli in order to stop the Austrians from hurrying up from the south. This could be done by leaving a covering corps, which the army would then file past to Novara, Turbigo, and Magenta. It was because Charles Albert did not take the precaution of covering himself to the south, that he was defeated.[1]

1 Ufficio Storico Stato Maggiore dell'Esercito, *La Guerra del 1859* vol I Documenti, Jomini to Napoleon III, page 220

Jomini's advice became the template for the next phase of the war, the Franco-Piedmontese offensive. The Austrians never had the initiative, but neither did the allied armies until they united. Even so, there was little combat other than a few skirmishes, and therefore the 2nd Army remained a coherent and substantial force. Napoleon III, Victor Emmanuel II, and their staffs met at Alessandria to discuss options. The French emperor did not immediately take the offensive, but dallied with probes and feints in the week following his arrival. He visited the battlefield of Marengo outside Alessandria. There, in 1800, his uncle had narrowly defeated the Austrians, sealing his victory in Italy.

Napoleon III failed to capitalize on Gyulai's redeployment, enabling the Austrian general to take stock of the situation and delay any further withdrawal across the Ticino to Lombardy. Gyulai deployed the divisions of VII Korps along the Sesia from Vercelli, held II and III Korps around Mortara, concentrated VIII Korps toward Pavia and moved V Korps halfway between Pavia and Mortara. All of this anticipated a flanking maneuver south of the Po. It is unclear at this point if the French actually intended on this approach or whether it was a feint. Marshal Baraguey d'Hilliers' I Corps advanced upon Tortona and then Voghera, where General Forey's division pushed forward toward Montebello.

This signaled an eastern movement toward Piacenza.

The advance from Voghera coincided with the movement of Garibaldi's command to the north. Giuseppe Garibaldi had accepted Cavour's offer in February. He met with King Victor Emmanuel II and pledged his loyalty to "Victor Emmanuel and Italy!" He then received a commission as a lieutenant general in the Piedmontese Army and was assigned to train the thousands of volunteers. Cavour and La Marmora decided to abandon Garibaldi's operations in the duchies, as the French intended on landing a corps under Prince Jérôme Napoleon in Tuscany. Cavour preferred this, as it meant a formal military force would "liberate" the duchies as opposed to a former Mazzinian and revolutionary volunteers.

Weeks before the war Garibaldi was given the opportunity to command a special volunteer unit to be deployed in the Lomellina to screen the Austrian advance. He chose 3,300 men from the 19,000 and organized them into three regiments, staffed by professional officers who had served with him in 1849. The Cacciatori delle Alpi were organized for war by the end of April, and dispatched to the Sesia. They saw little action

Napoleon III arrived at Genoa on May 12, 1859, aboard his flagship *Reine Hortense*, named for his mother. His arrival marked the end of the defensive phase of the war and the beginning of the offensive against the Austrians. (Anne S.K. Brown Military Collection, Brown University Library)

The infantry of the French Army were highly trained professionals. One-third of the regiments had been transported from Algeria where they had fought the various Berber tribesmen. A considerable number had also seen service in the Crimean War. (Anne S.K. Brown Military Collection, Brown University Library)

in the first weeks of the war and by May 20 La Marmora had redeployed them to the north. Garibaldi's orders were to operate on the far right of the Austrians and threaten their positions in the Lomellina, moving into Lombardy from the foothills of the Alps. The movement of French troops south of the Po, and of Garibaldi to the north, was meant to pressure Gyulai's strategic flanks.

Gyulai and his staff perceived the advance of French forces from Voghera as a precursor to a *manoeuvre sur la derrière*. General Urban's IX Korps, recently arrived at Piacenza, moved to preempt the French offensive. He was assisted by elements of Stadion's V Korps, which crossed the Po. On May 20, Forey's division engaged IX Korps at Montebello, in the first battle of the war. Three Piedmontese cavalry regiments, Aosta, Novara, and Montferrato, accompanied Forey's division.

At 11.30pm a squadron of the Novara Regiment spotted the advanced guard of Urban's corps at Casteggio, two miles east of Montebello. Forey's regiments were several miles to the west of Montebello, having just marched out of Voghera. The Aosta Regiment observed the advance of Feldmarschall Leutnant Paumgartten's division of V Korps four miles to the north. Piedmontese reconnaissance proved valuable, as it prevented Forey from marching directly into elements of two Austrian corps.

At 2.30pm Schaffgotsche's brigade (IX Korps) engaged Forey's lead brigade. Paumgartten's division (V Korps) moved to Urban's left. The cavalrymen of the Aosta Regiment and one battalion of French infantry occupied the Austrian forces on the flank, preventing them from participating in the battle. This allowed Forey to focus on the increasing pressure to his front. He deployed his two brigades, supported by Piedmontese cavalry and advanced upon the Austrians at Montebello. After three hours of hard fighting Urban believed that Forey's aggressiveness indicated that the rest of the French I Corps was en route. Having failed to stall Forey, he decided to withdraw from Montebello before nightfall.

The official report of the combat was sent by telegraph to Napoleon III at Alessandria on the morning of May 21:

The Austrians have attacked, on the 20th, with approximately 15,000 men the advanced posts of Marshal Baraguey d'Hilliers. They have been repulsed by Division Forey, which conducted itself admirably and liberated the village of Montebello, already famous [reference to the French victory in 1800], after a combat lasting four hours. The Piedmontese cavalry commanded by General de Sonnaz showed great energy equal to ours.

Forey's victory at Montebello caused concern in both Austrian and French headquarters. King Victor Emmanuel was informed of the engagement on the same day as Napoleon III, but kept an independent headquarters further north at Occimiano. Both the French

Feldmarschall Heinrich Hermann Josef Freiherr von Hess was the Chief of Staff of the Imperial Army. He served as Radetzky's chief of staff through the early 1850s when he was transferred to Vienna. Hess commanded the army of the German Confederation for a time. He hated Count Grünne and did not like Gyulai. (Anne S.K. Brown Military Collection, Brown University Library)

Feldmarschall Leutnant Ludwig von Benedek commanded the Austrian VIII Korps in 1859. He was an experienced officer who had spent many years prior to 1859 in Italy. He fought a see-saw battle with the Piedmontese at San Martino on June 24. (Peter Geymayer)

emperor and the Piedmontese king were pleased with the battle's outcome, but it indicated that Gyulai was not as passive as previously demonstrated. Indeed, he had clearly anticipated a maneuver south of the Po, thereby dispatching two corps to discourage the allied armies. The news of Urban and Stadion's repulse at Montebello was disconcerting at Gyulai's headquarters. Their fight did not obviate a *manoeuvre sur la derrière*, but indicated that the French were on the move south of the Po. Gyulai spread his corps further south, shifting Urban's IX Korps toward Piacenza, and Stadion's V Korps along the Po at Pavia. Feldmarschall Leutnant Benedek's VIII Korps took up positions at the confluence of the Po and Sesia, with Zobel's VII Korps to the north, covering the western approaches to Mortara from Palestro to Robbio and Candia. Liechtenstein's II Korps and Schwartzenberg's III Korps were positioned south of Mortara, to cover any allied advance upon Mortara, or counter movements south of the Po.

In the week following Montebello Napoleon III was too cautious. The Piedmontese could not act without the French, whose army represented the main strength at this point. Cialdini's 4th Division conducted a reconnaissance in force across the Sesia at Vercelli on May 21, finding little Austrian resistance. The imperial entourage and Victor Emmanuel and his staff traveled north to observe the state of Austrian defenses. They decided that the action at Montebello pinned Gyulai to the Po, leaving scant forces at Vercelli. The allies agreed to shift their center of operations from Alessandria to Casale and then Vercelli.

From May 27 through May 29 the French and Piedmontese armies conducted a lateral flank march. Using Piedmontese rail, Canrobert's III Corps and Niel's IV Corps

At the battle of Varese on May 26, the Cacciatori delle Alpi – 3,000 hand-picked volunteers who served under Garibaldi – repelled an attack by Austrian forces on their position. The Austrian assault was held by heavy fire and counterattack, and a regiment of Cacciatori assailed the Austrian left flank, forcing them to retreat. Garibaldi successfully led the Cacciatori in a campaign in the lower Alps that diverted more than 11,000 Austrians from the main theater of war in the Lomellina and Lombardy. (The Art Archive/Museo del Risorgimento Brescia/Gianni Dagli Orti)

were transported to Casale. The Piedmontese Army formed the allied right. General Enrico Cialdini's 4th Division became the tip of the spear of the Franco-Piedmontese offensive,

On May 28–29, 1859, the Franco-Piedmontese army conducted a strategic flank march, moving their axis of advance to the north. The advanced guard of the allied armies was composed of Cialdini's 4th Division that crossed the Sesia River at Vercelli and marched upon Palestro. (Anne S.K. Brown Military Collection, Brown University Library)

with Fanti's 2nd and Durando's 3rd marching in support. Saint-Angely's Imperial Guard Corps arrived at Casale, with Baraguey d'Hilliers' I Corps and MacMahon's II Corps along the Po northeast of Alessandria to prevent any Austrian countermeasures.

The Franco-Piedmontese offensive was further strengthened by Garibaldi's lightning operations in the Alps. Garibaldi's art of war rested upon doing what the enemy least expected. He believed in moving fast and conducting sharp actions to keep the enemy off balance. On May 23 he struck at Sesto Calende on the shores of Lake Maggiore, capturing a surprised Austrian garrison. Three days later he seized the town of Varese and repelled an Austrian counterattack. Garibaldi's achievement forced Gyulai to detach 11,000 men to the north under General Urban. From Varese, Garibaldi wound his way to San Fermo on May 27–28, brushing aside a blocking force and taking Como. Exhausted from days of marching and fighting, Garibaldi attacked the fortifications at Laveno on May 30, but could not capture it. He withdrew to Como to rest and refit. Urban failed to halt Garibaldi's movements though he had almost four times the number of soldiers.

On the day of the fighting at Laveno, the Franco-Piedmontese attacked the Austrian outposts at Palestro, opening the road to Mortara. The battle of Palestro involved two separate actions over a two-day period.

Cialdini's 4th Division crossed the Sesia at Vercelli followed by Durando's 3rd Division. Fanning out, Durando's regiments skirted to the northwest of Vinzaglio, while Cialdini marched on Palestro. Brigades Weigl and Dendorf of Zobel's VII Korps were responsible for this sector of the Sesia. Weigl held Palestro with most of Dendorf's command at Robbio. Several battalions from both were positioned to the north toward Vinzaglio, but did not have sufficient strength to oppose Durando's 1st Division (by this point Durando had replaced Castelborgo as 1st Division commander, with the 3rd Division being taken over by General Mollard). After three hours of fighting, Cialdini overran Palestro and his lead battalions pursued Weigl's troops halfway to Robbio.

Gyulai understood by the night of May 30 that the Piedmontese had established a large bridgehead across the Sesia. Four Piedmontese divisions were now holding Palestro, Vinzaglio, and Confienza. Marshal Canrobert's III Corps crossed the Sesia southwest of Palestro. General Niel's IV Corps continued to Vercelli followed by MacMahon's II Corps and the Imperial Guard. Hoping to force the Piedmontese and French back, Zobel counterattacked on May 31 with the two divisions of his VII Korps, reinforced by Feldmarschall Leutnant Szabo's brigade from II Korps.

Cialdini held Palestro with one brigade, as the other took position northeast of the town to prevent any Austrian attempt to flank it. As Canrobert's troops arrived, he fed them into the town to support Cialdini. By early afternoon French regiments had moved onto the flanks, extending the line. Austrian attacks were repulsed, but the decisive point came when the 3rd Zouaves crossed the canal and fell upon the Austrian left flank. King Victor Emmanuel II accompanied the Zouaves in their assault. The Austrian left was compromised and Zobel withdrew his brigades toward Robbio. The allied army was now in force on the east bank of the Sesia in the Lomellina.

The battle of Palestro convinced Gyulai that his army's current position between Mortara and Pavia meant an opened road to Milan if he did not withdraw across the Ticino. Gyulai contemplated concentrating his army at Mortara and advancing against Novara as Radetzky had done in 1849. He moved III Korps to Mortara and Zobel prepared for another attempt on Palestro. The rapid movement of the Franco-Piedmontese army, however, forced him

French divisions crossed the Sesia in support of the Piedmontese attack at Palestro. The 3rd Zouaves were attached to Cialdini's 4th Division, while the remainder of Canrobert's III Corps deployed in and around the town. (Anne S.K. Brown Military Collection, Brown University Library)

to abandon that thought. Applying Jomini's advice, the divisions of the Piedmontese Army comprised the blocking force, permitting the French army to march unimpeded to Novara. The day after Palestro four French corps were in line of march extending from Vercelli to Novara, protected by 40,000 Piedmontese.

Despite considerable contemporary and historical criticism, Gyulai anticipated an allied advance upon Milan. He remained unclear, however, as to the exact approach. Gyulai was confounded by lack of field experience and paralyzed by indecision. It took a day or two before he accepted that the events at Palestro were not a feint. Even so, Gyulai still worried that the French intended to move south of the Po, and held VIII and IX Korps in position from Pavia to Piacenza. This was foolish, as there had been no actions south of the Po after Montebello, and the only French forces in the vicinity of Pavia were General d'Autemarre's division of V Corps. Although he was posted briefly at Voghera, there were no probes against Pavia or east toward Piacenza. It is important to note that, despite possessing substantial cavalry, Gyulai never conducted reconnaissance to determine the direction of the actual allied advance.

Gyulai's situation was further complicated by the arrival of Feldmarschall Heinrich von Hess from Vienna. He and the emperor were furious at Gyulai's mishandling of the campaign. Franz Josef and Hess had left Vienna for Verona on May 29. They arrived in time to receive news of the battle of Palestro and observe the retreat of the 2nd Army. The emperor and his chief of staff believed Gyulai mishandled the situation, and when the 2nd Army withdrew into Lombardy, they worried that he would not assume a defensive position, but continue west toward the Quadrilateral. There is no evidence that Gyulai had such a plan, and it appears that he did indeed intend to defend the Ticino. Nevertheless, Hess arrived at Gyulai's headquarters at Abbiategrasso on June 3, and presented the emperor's demand to take all action necessary to defend the frontier.

Gyulai held the line from Magenta to Abbiategrasso, five miles to the south. Unknown to the allies, the 2nd Army benefited from the recent arrival of the Austrian I Korps from Bohemia. Feldmarschall Leutnant Clam Gallas moved his divisions into Magenta as a blocking force reinforced by Feldmarschall Leutnant Mensdorff's cavalry reserve and elements of II Korps. The VII Korps was at Gyulai's headquarters at Abbiategrasso, with III and V Korps several miles to the south, covering the secondary approach to Milan from Vigevano. At this point Gyulai had no reason to maintain VIII and IX Korps to guard the Po. It was abundantly clear that the allied armies were not attempting a *manoeuvre sur la derrière*. Gyulai's failure to call these corps closer to Milan or Magenta by June 3 can be attributed to Hess, who possessed the authority to order it. Yet, it was not done and Hess' presence further affected Gyulai's ability to command. General Mollinary, who commanded a brigade with the army, recalled that Gyulai was terribly nervous around Colonel Kuhn,

Opposite: the battle of Magenta was the first major engagement between the French and Austrian armies in 1859. Feldzeugmeister Gyulai was outmaneuvered in the Lomellina, and tried to defend the Lombard frontier, but was again outflanked when General MacMahon's reinforced corps crossed the Ticino to the north and compromised the Austrian positions at Magenta.

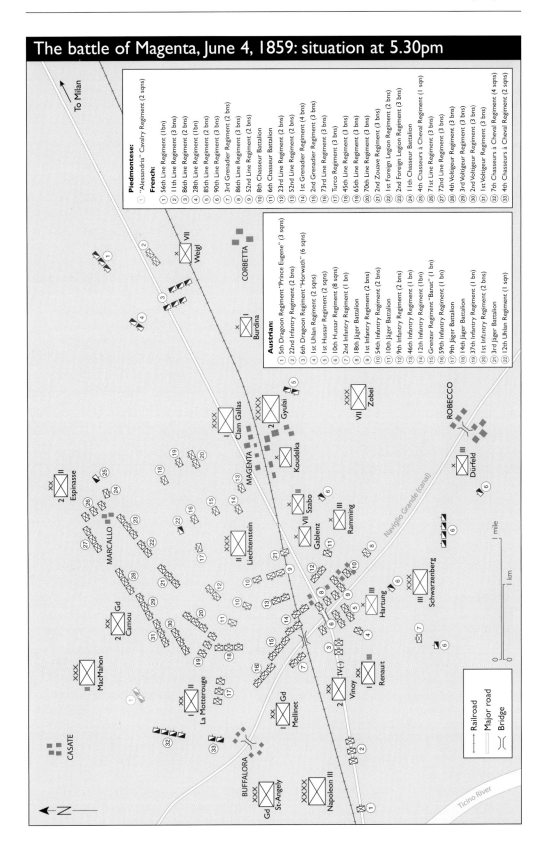

The battle of Magenta, June 4, 1859: situation at 5.30pm

Piedmontese:
1. "Alessandria" Cavalry Regiment (2 sqns)

French:
1. 56th Line Regiment (1bn)
2. 11th Line Regiment (3 bns)
3. 86th Line Regiment (2 bns)
4. 28th Line Regiment (1bn)
5. 85th Line Regiment (2 bns)
6. 90th Line Regiment (3 bns)
7. 3rd Grenadier Regiment (2 bns)
8. 86th Line Regiment (3 bns)
9. 52nd Line Regiment (2 bns)
10. 8th Chasseur Battalion
11. 6th Chasseur Battalion
12. 23rd Line Regiment (2 bns)
13. 52nd Line Regiment (2 bns)
14. 1st Grenadier Regiment (4 bns)
15. 2nd Grenadier Regiment (3 bns)
16. 73rd Line Regiment (3 bns)
17. Turco Regiment (3 bns)
18. 45th Line Regiment (3 bns)
19. 65th Line Regiment (3 bns)
20. 70th Line Regiment (3 bns)
21. 2nd Zouave Regiment (3 bns)
22. 1st Foreign Legion Regiment (2 bns)
23. 2nd Foreign Legion Regiment (3 bns)
24. 11th Chasseur Battalion
25. 4th Chasseurs à Cheval Regiment (1 sqn)
26. 71st Line Regiment (3 bns)
27. 72nd Line Regiment (3 bns)
28. 4th Voltigeur Regiment (3 bns)
29. 3rd Voltigeur Regiment (3 bns)
30. 2nd Voltigeur Regiment (3 bns)
31. 1st Voltigeur Regiment (3 bns)
32. 7th Chasseurs à Cheval Regiment (4 sqns)
33. 4th Chasseurs à Cheval Regiment (2 sqns)

Austrian:
1. 5th Dragoon Regiment "Prince Eugene" (3 sqns)
2. 22nd Infantry Regiment (2 bns)
3. 6th Dragoon Regiment "Horwath" (6 sqns)
4. 1st Uhlan Regiment (2 sqns)
5. 1st Hussar Regiment (2 sqns)
6. 10th Hussar Regiment (8 sqns)
7. 2nd Infantry Regiment (1 bn)
8. 18th Jäger Battalion
9. 1st Infantry Regiment (2 bns)
10. 54th Infantry Regiment (2 bns)
11. 10th Jäger Battalion
12. 9th Infantry Regiment (2 bns)
13. 46th Infantry Regiment (1bn)
14. 12th Infantry Regiment (1bn)
15. Grenzer Regiment "Banat" (1 bn)
16. 59th Infantry Regiment (1 bn)
17. 9th Jäger Battalion
18. 14th Jäger Battalion
19. 37th Infantry Regiment (1 bn)
20. 1st Infantry Regiment (2 bns)
21. 3rd Jäger Battalion
22. 12th Uhlan Regiment (1 sqn)

To Milan

CASATE

BUFFALORA

MacMahon

Espinasse

MARCALLO

Gd Camou

La Motterouge

2 Gd Mellinet

Gd St-Angely

Napoleon III

Vinoy

Renaut

Clam Gallas

MAGENTA

Gyulai

Koudelka

Liechtenstein

Szabo

Gablenz

Ramming

Hartung

Schwarzenberg

Zobel

Burdina

CORBETTA

Weigl

ROBECCO

Dürfeld

Naviglio Grande (canal)

Ticino River

Railroad

Major road

Bridge

1 mile

1 km

N

The second day of the battle of Palestro witnessed the attempt by Zobel's VII Korps to retake the town from the Piedmontese. King Victor Emmanuel, leading the French regiment, 3rd Zouaves, crossed the canal west of Palestro, and took the Austrians in the flank. After the battle the Zouaves declared the king an honorary corporal of the regiment. (Anne S.K. Brown Military Collection, Brown University Library)

his chief of staff and a close friend of Hess. No doubt the physical presence of both Hess and Kuhn further unsettled the irresolute Feldzeugmeister, and perhaps helps to explain Gyulai's lethargy.

The battle of Magenta, June 4, 1859

The Austrians held a good defensive position at Magenta. The bridges over the Ticino from Turbigo to Vigevano were blown, but this provided only a temporary delay. The Ticino created many small islands in its center, and while it formed a clear border between Lombardy and Piedmont, the true defensive line was found along the canal that flowed parallel to the Ticino. The Naviglio Grande (Large Canal), constructed on a raised bank a mile and a half from the Ticino, created a formidable obstacle. The speed of current and depth of water made it impossible to traverse except at four established bridges. Pontoons could not be employed across the canal owing to the nature of their banks.

The Austrian army in the vicinity of Magenta numbered 41,000 men. This included I and II Korps and one division of VII Korps, plus Mensdorff's cavalry reserve. South of Gyulai's headquarters at Abbiategrasso stood Schwarzenberg's III Korps and the other division of VII Korps, Sternak's, with 27,000 men. Stadion's V Korps was too distant to participate in the action. Gyulai therefore had 68,000 men in range of the battlefield on June 4. When examining allied operations and Gyulai's fears and mistakes through June 3, it appears that he believed the Franco-Piedmontese might strike at either Magenta or across the Ticino from Vigevano. A headlong advance by the French into Magenta could be held. An attack from Vigevano could be delayed while forces from Magenta, V and VIII Korps could be called upon. Allied movements clearly forced Gyulai to overthink the threats and disperse his army. The French and Piedmontese did not oblige Gyulai and disaster was averted only because the allies were unaware of the arrival of I Korps at Milan and its immediate deployment to Magenta.

The pursuit of the 2nd Army from June 1 through June 3 was swift, but the French and Piedmontese lost contact with their enemy. As the main allied forces advanced directly toward Milan, they anticipated a strong defense around Magenta. Napoleon III and his staff intended to take Magenta from front and flank, clearing the road to Milan. The French had slightly more than 50,000 men on hand, with Fanti's 2nd Division adding another 12,000. Much of the allied army remained strung out on the line of march and this prevented rapid concentration at Magenta. The two armies were evenly matched in numbers, but only if Gyulai moved his corps quickly to the point of contact.

General Camou with a division of the Guard Voltigeurs, followed by MacMahon's II Corps and Fanti's 2nd Division, arrived at Turbigo, five miles northwest of Magenta, in an attempt to outflank Austrian positions, making the defense of the Naviglio Grande untenable. Camou's division crossed the Ticino by boat between 2 and 3am on June 4. With the right bank secure, the French laid a pontoon bridge. MacMahon's divisions were ordered to precede Fanti's 2nd Division, which followed by midday.

The French Imperial Guard Corps marched across the pontoon bridge on the Ticino, led by Mellinet's division of Guard Grenadiers along the main rail line and road to Milan. The 2nd Grenadier Regiment moved against the canal bridge at Buffalora, and the rest of the division headed directly upon the Ponte Nuovo west of Magenta by 1.30pm. Elements of Marshal Canrobert's III Corps, followed by Niel's IV Corps, came up behind the Guard

Corps, but were delayed by the traffic jam developing at the bridge over the Ticino. The Austrians had set charges but they failed to demolish the structure. Although damaged, it was usable. The French threw a pontoon bridge across to facilitate their movement, but it still required time to move the corps forward.

MacMahon's divisions advanced along parallel routes to Magenta. General La Motterouge's division (II Corps) marched via Cuggiono upon the canal bridges at Bernante and Buffalora. Camou's Guard division followed. General Espinasse's division (II Corps) took the road to the east from Buscate toward Inveruono, which placed it due north of Magenta.

Napoleon III expected MacMahon's movement on Buffalora to coincide with the arrival of the 2nd Grenadier Regiment. Exact coordination was impossible, as MacMahon had been out of touch since the previous evening. At noon the advanced

The French advance across the Ticino included two flanking maneuvers. The 3rd Grenadier Regiment attacked the town of Buffalora across the Grande Naviglio. The town was heartily defended by Austrian battalions that made the French Guard pay dearly. (Anne S.K. Brown Military Collection, Brown University Library)

guard of La Motterouge's division encountered Austrian battalions in Buffalora and fell back to the main body. MacMahon did not order an immediate assault as he was surprised by the appearance of an Austrian brigade (Koudelka) marching from Magenta into the fields east of Buffalora. It was at this moment that MacMahon realized that he faced more than an Austrian rear guard. Koudelka's battalions were part of Liechtenstein's II Korps. MacMahon responded by deploying his divisions to cover the line from Casate due east, with Camou's division in reserve and Fanti's 2nd Division in the rear, still crossing at Turbigo.

Along the Naviglio from Buffalora to Magenta, the Imperial Guard Corps made contact with the Austrians who had settled into the stone houses of the towns and had placed artillery to defend the bridges. The 2nd Grenadiers were engaged in a serious combat at Buffalora, while their comrades in the 1st and 3rd Grenadiers fought to seize a foothold on the right bank of the Naviglio. The fighting intensified through 2pm, when the Guard Zouaves found boats downstream

The Austrians had attempted to slow the Franco-Piedmontese armies by destroying the bridges on the Ticino. In most cases, the masonry construction prevented the complete destruction of the bridges and infantry was able to cross. (Anne S.K. Brown Military Collection, Brown University Library)

Opposite: the battle of Solferino decided the war of 1859. Although it was a meeting engagement, the French, Piedmontese, and Austrian armies fought throughout the day over three key positions: the town of Solferino, the Campo di Medole, and the heights of San Martino. The Austrians lost the town by the afternoon, while their attacks on the Campo di Medole were repulsed with heavy loss.

and crossed the canal. The Zouaves established a tenuous bridgehead on the right bank. Napoleon III was confused by both the strength of resistance and the failure of MacMahon's attack to materialize. He was unaware of the combat north of the town. The emperor was equally frustrated by the slow pace of Canrobert's corps, which was to move in support of the Guard, but only appeared at 2.30pm.

French and Piedmontese movements on June 4 suffered terribly from cluttered roads. The allied army had benefited in May from the use of Piedmontese railroads. The flank march to Vercelli and the advance to Novara were achieved largely by rail movement. From Novara to Magenta, the army did not rely upon railroad for logistical support but hundreds of wagons accompanied each corps and division. When MacMahon and the Guard Corps moved on Magenta, the roads behind were blocked, particularly when substantial Austrian resistance halted the attack. Canrobert, Niel, and Fanti had to navigate their routes by moving around the

The battle of Solferino, June 24, 1859: situation at 12pm

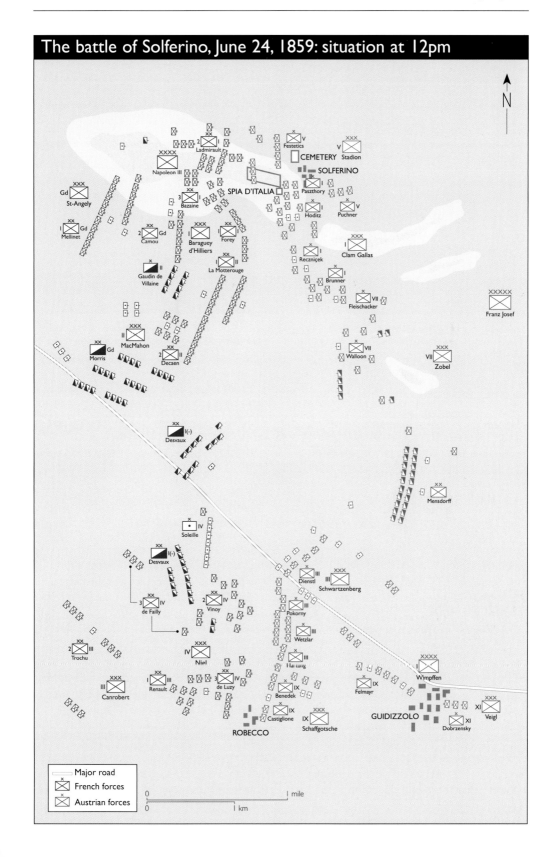

The French assault on Magenta from the north and west succeeded in squeezing the Austrian forces. By evening the Guard Zouaves and regiments from IV Corps pushed into the town. (Anne S.K. Brown Military Collection, Brown University Library)

stalled supply trains. This was the only reason for their delay.

Austrian general Clam Gallas' orders stated that he should withdraw if faced by a determined enemy. Despite the ferocity of combat on the Naviglio he held his position and informed Gyulai of the French attack. The Feldzeugmeister received the news and sent Schwarzenberg's III Korps from Robecco to Magenta, along the west bank of the canal. This attack on the French right flank threatened Napoleon's position between the Ponte Vecchio and Ponte Nuovo. Gyulai alerted Stadion at V Korps, sending him to Magenta, although these reinforcements could not reach the town in time.

At 1.30pm Gyulai and Hess arrived at Magenta to observe the threat first hand. By that time MacMahon had pulled back his advanced guard to prepare a formal assault on the Austrian line running east from Buffalora. The French Guard Grenadiers had yet to gain position on the east bank of the Naviglio at Buffalora; therefore neither Gyulai nor Hess properly assessed the danger of their position. Mensdorff's cavalry, on the far right, did

nothing more than posture against MacMahon, while the brigades of VII Korps took post in reserve to the south and west of Magenta.

As the attack by Schwarzenberg's III Korps materialized on the French right, Canrobert's lead brigade arrived and was immediately sent into action. The fighting on the right degenerated into a firefight, but this worked to the French advantage. General Vinoy's division from IV Corps skirted the combat on the right and reinforced the Guard on the Naviglio by 5.30pm. From 3.30 through 5.30pm MacMahon launched a coordinated attack against the Austrian I and II Korps. Espinasse's division and Camou's Guard pushed the Austrian battalions back as La Motterouge's division cleared Buffalora from the north, and moved into line with Camou. The attack was a clear success as La Motterouge's battalions made contact with Vinoy's regiments on the right bank of the canal.

The Austrian position was lost by 6.30pm. The battalions were in good order although bloodied, and this permitted Gyulai to conduct a fighting withdrawal to the southeast toward V Korps. The French divisions fought their way into Magenta and beyond. The 9th Bersaglieri Battalion, leading Fanti's 2nd Division, arrived on MacMahon's left by 5pm, but it required another three hours for the division to steer a course around the long line of wagons. Their arrival prevented Mensdorff's cavalry and Feldmarschall Leutnant Rezniçek's and Feldmarschall Leutnant Weigel's infantry brigades from attacking MacMahon's left, and thus compromising the French position.

By 10pm the Austrian 2nd Army was withdrawing in good order toward Abbiategrasso and the southeast. The direction of the retreat opened the gateway to Milan. The Austrians had committed 58,000 to the battle, compared to the 54,000 for the French and 12,000 for Fanti's division. Casualties were high, but not excessive considering the intensity of combat. The French suffered 4,500 killed and wounded compared to 9,700 Austrians. It is surprising that the French did not lose more men in view of the strong Austrian position.

The defeat at Magenta spelled the end for Gyulai. He withdrew his army to the Chiese River east of Milan, and resigned on June 16. The Austrian army comprising six infantry corps and two cavalry corps was then divided into two armies. Feldzeugmeister Count Wimpffen commanded the 1st Army (II, III, IX, XI Korps and cavalry reserve) and General der Kavallerie Count Schlick replaced Gyulai in the 2nd Army (I, V, VII, VIII Korps and cavalry reserve). The Austrians continued their retreat to the Mincio River.

On June 18 the Emperor Franz Josef took personal command of both armies and the subsequent conduct of the campaign. From Verona, he had the security of the Quadrilateral fortresses. The Austrian strategic situation was reminiscent of 1848. Outlying Austrian troops at Pavia, Piacenza, and the Papal States were recalled to the army. Franz Josef, however, was not Radetzky. Impatient and desiring to strike back, the emperor ordered his armies across the Mincio to the Chiese on June 23. The next day his army unexpectedly collided with the French and Piedmontese at Solferino–San Martino. The battle decided the war.

Solferino and San Martino, June 24, 1859

Napoleon III and Victor Emmanuel II entered Milan on June 8. Their triumph encouraged

After the victory at Magenta, the Austrians abandoned Lombardy. Victor Emmanuel II and Napoleon III made a triumphal entrance into Milan and then Brescia a few days later. (Anne S.K. Brown Military Collection, Brown University Library)

revolutions in Tuscany, Parma, and Modena. Cavour had anticipated this in the fall of 1858. In order to ensure the moderation of these revolutions Prince Jérôme Napoleon's V Corps landed at Livorno on May 23–25 and entered Florence a week later. Not long after the entrance into Milan, Prince Napoleon was ordered to send one division to the city of Parma, and his other across the Apennines to Modena. Autemarre's division at Voghera was finally dispatched to Piacenza after the departure of the Austrian garrison.

The Franco-Piedmontese army continued its easterly movement into Venetia. Piedmontese and French cavalry maintained contact with the Austrian rearguard until they crossed the Chiese. Thereafter both armies broke off contact. The Austrians spent the week preceding the counteroffensive reorganizing the command structure and receiving reinforcements and supplies.

The French assaulted Solferino throughout the morning, as the Austrians took position in the walled cemetery, church, and convent of the small town. (The Art Archive/Museo del Risorgimento Turin)

Unlike the first six weeks of the war, the allied armies now began to experience significant logistical problems. The tracks on the rail bridge over the Ticino had been dismantled, and needed repair before trains could operate between Genoa, Turin, and Milan. The French Navy shipped locomotives to Genoa, as Piedmontese rail capacity was already at its maximum. Finally, a siege train left Marseilles and Toulon for Genoa where it could be transported via rail into Lombardy.

On June 22 the allied armies were ordered across the Chiese to the Mincio. Four of the five Piedmontese divisions (37,000 men) formed the left wing of the army. The French I and II corps advanced in the center, with the Imperial Guard in reserve (52,000 men). III and IV corps composed the right wing (44,000 men). Simultaneously, and unknown to the allied monarchs, Franz Josef moved his armies across the Mincio on June 23. Wimpffen's 1st Army (57,000 men) held the Austrian left, and the 2nd Army (45,500) the

center. The left wing included Benedek's VIII Korps (20,000) with two brigades of V Korps (8,500) in the gap between the left and center. Both armies advanced along the same routes unaware that they were converging around Medole, Solferino, and San Martino.

The battle of Solferino–San Martino developed into three separate actions of which Medole and Solferino formed one battle, and San Martino a second. The battle of Solferino involved French and Austrian armies, while San Martino was fought between the Piedmontese and the Austrians. These two actions have developed into distinct battle narratives, but they resulted from the same operational plans.

Solferino, June 24, 1859

The battlefield of Solferino is divided into two distinct geographic features. The town of Solferino is on the eastern side of a small mountain with a tower and medieval walls. Just north of Solferino the land consists of fields and sharp rolling hills until San Martino and northwest to Madonna della Scoperta. South of Solferino, the land opens into the broad plain of Campo di Medole, which extends several miles. The fighting

developed into separate actions around each of these two geographical features.

The first engagements of the day occurred at 5am west of Solferino. Marshal Baraguey d'Hilliers' I Corps began its march from Castiglione at 3am. French cavalry located Austrian troops from Stadion's V Korps west of the heights before 5am. General Ladmirault's division, supported by Forey's brigades on the right, pushed the Austrian outposts back to Solferino. By 8am the French held a line along the heights parallel to Solferino and its environs. Stadion's brigades took position in the cemetery and town with a brigade deployed to the north toward Madonna della Scoperta. For the next three hours the divisions of I Corps fought for control of Solferino. Fighting was intense, and the walls around the town and the cemetery provided solid cover for Austrian battalions. Stadion received reinforcements from Clam Gallas' I Korps but Napoleon III fed the Imperial Guard divisions into the combat and by 2pm the cemetery and town were surrounded. General Bazaine's division of I Corps was committed to the action, finally taking Solferino and the cemetery.

To the south, MacMahon's II Corps, supported by two divisions of cavalry, pressed the Austrian VII Korps at San Cassiano. The struggle for control over the northern part of

Stadion's V Korps held the ground from the town of Solferino to Madonna della Scoperta to the north. The Piedmontese 1st Division, including the Guards Brigade, fought throughout the day to take the latter town and hill from the Austrians. (Anne S.K. Brown Military Collection, Brown University Library)

the Campo di Medole continued through the morning, as the winner would threaten the positions at Solferino. Not until 2pm did La Motterouge's division and the Imperial Guard cavalry succeed in breaking the Austrian line, thereby threatening the headquarters of the 1st Army at Cavriana.

Further south still, on the Campo di Medole, General Niel's IV Corps along with elements of Canrobert's III Corps engaged the 2nd Army. Three divisions of French cavalry maintained the line from Niel's left wing to the French center. The Austrian cavalry reserve under Mensdorff was deployed opposite, and only committed by mid-afternoon. Thus, the fighting in the south was isolated from the actions at Solferino.

Niel was at a significant disadvantage. He commanded three and a half divisions against three Austrian corps (III, IX, and XI). The first engagement began in the early morning hours and had intensified by 8am when the weight of the Austrian attack fell upon Niel's divisions. Niel formed a grand battery to support his corps. The French

Taken from the tower on the heights overlooking Solferino, this is the view from Napoleon III's perspective by midday, toward Stadion's V Corps. (Author)

rifled artillery did murder, and their range and accuracy were vital to holding the line. By early afternoon, the Austrian attack had failed and Niel pushed beyond Robecco and Casa Nova halfway to Guidizzolo.

At 3pm General Renault's division of Canrobert's III Corps arrived at Robecco. Niel, now reinforced, launched a coordinated attack on Guidizzolo. Austrian brigades from III and XI Korps were sent forward and stalled the French assault. Indecisive fighting continued for the next two hours. Exhausted, Niel withdrew his divisions, having failed to take the town. The ability of the 2nd Army to halt the French offensive in the south did not mitigate the loss of Solferino and the battle to the north. Franz Josef and his staff concluded that the battle was lost, and ordered a general withdrawal to Mincio by early evening. Sporadic fighting continued into the night as the Austrian rear-guard delayed any French pursuit.

San Martino and Madonna della Scoperta, June 24, 1859

The Piedmontese Army formed the left wing of the allied advance across the Chiese. Cialdini's division was detached to relieve Garibaldi's Cacciatori delle Alpi who had fought at San Fermo and Tre Ponti, securing Brescia. Victor Emmanuel kept a separate headquarters throughout the campaign, and while the coordinated staffs were with Napoleon III at Montichiari, Victor Emmanuel established his royal headquarters at Lonato. The 3rd Division, now under General Mollard, marched along the rail line from Rivoltella and then turned south toward Pozzolengo. Immediately behind was Cucchiari's 5th Division at Lonato. The 1st Division under Durando, which included the Granatieri Brigade – the Royal Guard – was also at Lonato. They moved in conjunction with Fanti's 2nd Division, to fill the gap between the French army marching from Castiglione upon Cavriana and the Piedmontese divisions to their left.

The Piedmontese divisions were still at full strength. Only Cialdini's 4th Division had been engaged in significant combat at Palestro the previous month. French and Austrian armies received some reinforcement, but not those regiments that fought at Magenta. On June 24, the fighting at Madonna della Scoperta and San Martino involved forces on both sides that had yet to see combat after almost eight weeks of war.

At 7am the advanced guard of the 5th Division under Raffaele Cadorna (father of the future Italian marshal) moved south along the road from Rivoltella to Pozzolengo. As it approached the *cascina* (walled farm) of Pontecello, Brigade Lippert of Benedek's VIII Korps surprised it. Cadorna's battalions withdrew in good order upon the reconnaissance battalions of Mollard's 3rd Division, north of San Martino church. The Austrian brigade took up position at the church and along the hill upon which the church was situated. Not far behind was Brigade Reichlin, which took post to Lippert's left. Alerted to the presence of Austrian forces in the direction of Pozzolengo, Mollard deployed the Cuneo Brigade to attack.

The advanced guards of the 3rd and 5th divisions had marched a solid two hours in advance of their parent formations. This provided proper reconnaissance of the road ahead, but meant that the Piedmontese main body was strung out on the line of march. The Cuneo Brigade reached the field, but its supporting formation, the Pinerolo Brigade, was too distant. Cucchiari's division was at least two more hours from the field. Mollard worried that if he waited for his entire division to arrive, the Austrians would have time to secure their foothold on the only prominent elevation in the area. He thus ordered an attack at 9am.

Feldmarschall Leutnant Benedek's VIII Korps had camped at Pozzolengo, and the brigades near Pontecello formed his advanced guard. His corps was the extreme right of the Austrian army. Benedek's orders were to conduct a flank march from Pozzolengo against the French left somewhere between the Mincio and Chiese. Benedek was not expecting to make contact with Piedmontese forces that day. Ludwig Benedek was perhaps the best corps commander with the Imperial Army. He had served in Italy for many years under Radetzky and then for a short while in Galicia before returning to Lombardy. Benedek's brigades had been reshuffled, and reinforced to six brigades from the standard four. At 9am, however, the two attached brigades were still en route to San Martino.

The Cuneo Brigade's assault overlapped the Austrian position from Columbare to San Martino. The Piedmontese advanced upon the

The view from the Austrian perspective of V Korps looking toward the Spia d'Italia. The village of Solferino is in the center of the picture. (Author)

heights backed by three batteries, but their formation lacked depth. The Austrian brigades were equally supported by artillery, but the Cuneo Brigade's regiments swept up the hill and pushed the Austrians toward Pozzolengo. Benedek understood that this was more than a reconnaissance in force, and committed much of his corps to the action. The timely arrival of Brigade Berger from Pozzolengo reversed the Piedmontese success and sent the regiments of the Cuneo Brigade in confusion beyond their original position.

Benedek had three brigades along the hill, with his left resting upon two *cascine*, Columbare and the larger Contracania. In the center, the Austrians held San Martino, no more than a few buildings and the church. The Austrian left wrapped slightly around the hill. Mollard attended to his shaken troops as the recently arrived Casale Brigade from Cucchiari's division moved to the attack at 10.45am. The assault began well enough, but as the Austrian line was taken, Benedek directed Feldmarschall Leutnant Philipoviç's brigade to the far right flank. The Austrians turned the Piedmontese position, forcing the Casale Brigade to retreat with significant losses.

At noon Cucchiari made a second attempt on the hill with his full division. Once more, proper artillery support and the discipline of

The battle of San Martino, June 24, 1859: situation at 7pm

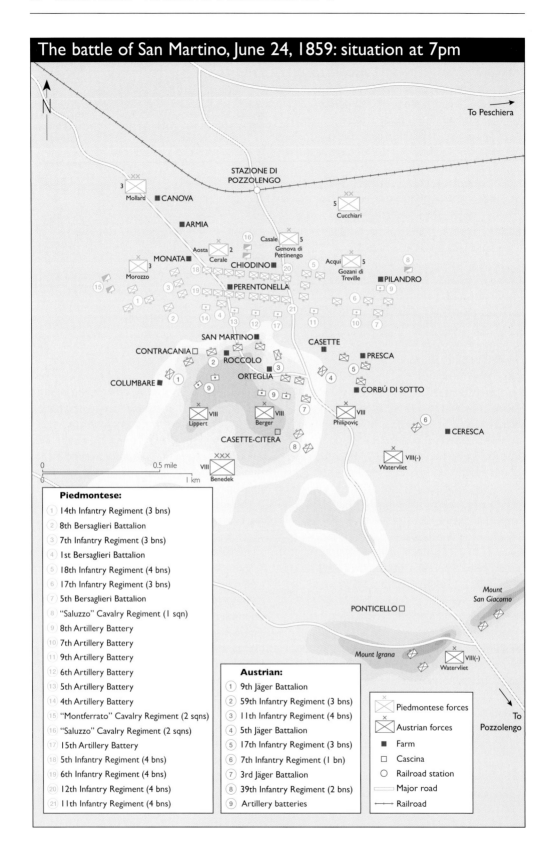

Piedmontese:

1. 14th Infantry Regiment (3 bns)
2. 8th Bersaglieri Battalion
3. 7th Infantry Regiment (3 bns)
4. 1st Bersaglieri Battalion
5. 18th Infantry Regiment (4 bns)
6. 17th Infantry Regiment (3 bns)
7. 5th Bersaglieri Battalion
8. "Saluzzo" Cavalry Regiment (1 sqn)
9. 8th Artillery Battery
10. 7th Artillery Battery
11. 9th Artillery Battery
12. 6th Artillery Battery
13. 5th Artillery Battery
14. 4th Artillery Battery
15. "Montferrato" Cavalry Regiment (2 sqns)
16. "Saluzzo" Cavalry Regiment (2 sqns)
17. 15th Artillery Battery
18. 5th Infantry Regiment (4 bns)
19. 6th Infantry Regiment (4 bns)
20. 12th Infantry Regiment (4 bns)
21. 11th Infantry Regiment (4 bns)

Austrian:

1. 9th Jäger Battalion
2. 59th Infantry Regiment (3 bns)
3. 11th Infantry Regiment (4 bns)
4. 5th Jäger Battalion
5. 17th Infantry Regiment (3 bns)
6. 7th Infantry Regiment (1 bn)
7. 3rd Jäger Battalion
8. 39th Infantry Regiment (2 bns)
9. Artillery batteries

Piedmontese forces
Austrian forces
■ Farm
□ Cascina
○ Railroad station
— Major road
+—+ Railroad

Piedmontese infantry took them to the hill, but Benedek had reinforced his position with massed batteries, which decimated Cucchiari's battalions. Benedek committed Brigade Waterfliet, thereby extending his right, threatening Cucchiari's flank. The firepower from Austrian guns and the turning movement unglued the Piedmontese division, routing them. Cucchiari's shattered regiments were finally halted north of the rail line almost two miles to the rear.

A lull settled on the battlefield for much of the afternoon. Although Mollard's second formation, the Pinerolo Brigade, arrived by 1.30pm, he held it back in case of an Austrian offensive. Cucchiari and Mollard spent the next several hours restoring order among their divisions and preparing for a coordinated assault. They also requested reinforcements, which were dispatched from Fanti's 2nd Division to the rear between San Martino and Madonna della Scoperta.

The fighting at Madonna della Scoperta followed a similar pattern to that at San Martino. Two brigades from Stadion's V Korps held the ground around the town and its prominent hill. The Savoia Brigade from Durando's 1st Division made several attacks on the town throughout the day, without success. By late afternoon, however, an assault by the Granatiere Brigade (the Royal Guard) took the hill and the outskirts of the town. By this time, the Austrians had lost Solferino to the southeast and Stadion's battalions gradually withdrew.

At 7.30pm Mollard and Cucchiari began their final assault on San Martino. The Aosta Brigade from Fanti's 2nd Division joined Mollard, while Cucchiari brought his two brigades into line. Benedek saw the serried ranks of Piedmontese with their artillery lining the front. As the Piedmontese attack came in, Benedek determined to conduct a

Opposite: the battle of San Martino was fought on the northern part of the Solferino battlefield. The Piedmontese Army encountered Feldmarschall Leutnant Benedek's VIII Korps near Pozzolengo. Throughout the day the Piedmontese divisions of Mollard and Cucchiari made numerous assaults on the Austrian positions along the line of the San Martino heights.

Contracania was a walled farmhouse held by the Austrians during the battle of San Martino. Its position anchored the Austrian left and cost the Piedmontese dearly to capture. (Author)

fighting withdrawal having received word of the Austrian retreat from Solferino. The Piedmontese divisions made their attack as the Austrian battalions along the line fought a delaying action. Benedek managed to extricate his corps. The Piedmontese stormed the *cascina* Contracania, and took San Martino and the church. Upon reaching the crest, however, they halted, exhausted.

The taking of San Martino marked the end of the last major fighting on June 24. Skirmishing between armies continued for several hours, but Franz Josef had lost the battle. The Habsburg army withdrew to the east bank of the Mincio, and then the Adige, returning to the security of the Quadrilateral. Napoleon III and Victor Emmanuel II appreciated their hard-fought victory, but it had been extremely costly. The Piedmontese Army had suffered their greatest casualties in any single engagement of their war: some 5,000 killed and wounded. The French had lost slightly more than twice that number and of the Austrian forces 22,000 were killed or wounded. The cost of war had a dramatic impact on Henri Dunant, a Swiss businessman, who observed the battle. His shock at the carnage led to his subsequent creation of the International Red Cross in 1863.

After the repulse of the Austrian assaults on Niel's IV Corps, the French counterattacked in the afternoon toward Austrian headquarters at Cavriana. Austrian battalions and artillery prevented the French from taking the town. (Anne S.K. Brown Military Collection, Brown University Library)

The position of the allied armies at the end of June was reminiscent of Charles Albert's in 1848. The difference however, was in the availability of resources, supplies, and manpower. The Piedmontese laid siege to Peschiera, and the French siege train was transported to Lombardy to be employed against Mantua. Yet, Franz Josef and Napoleon III had separately concluded that the war was at an end. For the Austrian emperor, the personal impact of defeat threatened the larger empire. For the French emperor, the devastation of battle and the threat of the war expanding to Germany compelled him to seek a separate peace with Austria. General Fleury, Napoleon's aide de camp, secretly traveled to Verona on 6 July. He met with Franz Josef and Feldmarschall Hess to discuss terms. A verbal agreement established an armistice that was formalized on July 8 when the Austrian emperor and Napoleon III met at Villafranca. The Peace of Villafranca effectively concluded the campaign of 1859. Unknown to the participants, this marked the conclusion of merely the first phase of the Second War of Italian Unification.

Giuseppe Garibaldi and the Thousand, May–August 1860

Giuseppe Garibaldi's campaign in Sicily in 1860 is generally understood in a rather romantic context. Garibaldi had many admirers by 1860, including Alexandre Dumas, the famed French author. Dumas was commissioned by Garibaldi to write his biography, and the volume he produced possessed a classic Dumas flair. The legend of Garibaldi often warped perceptions of the actual events. While it is true that Garibaldi led 1,089 volunteers on an expedition to Sicily, he did not conquer the island by charisma alone. The facts are quite dramatic, and lend themselves to a romanticization of the campaign. What makes Garibaldi's campaign so impressive is how quickly the Kingdom of the Two Sicilies fell to his forces. The kingdom had an enormous army and a navy much larger than that of Piedmont–Sardinia. The fall of Sicily in August 1860 and the subsequent disintegration of the regime reflected its significant weakness, the limitations of its armed forces, and the indirect role played by Cavour and Piedmont–Sardinia in affecting the collapse of their neighbor to the south.

Giuseppe Garibaldi resigned his commission in the Piedmontese Army after the Peace of Villafranca. He, like Cavour, perceived Napoleon III's actions as a betrayal of the Italian cause. Nevertheless, in the spring of 1860 Francesco Crispi and Giuseppe La Masa, Sicilian revolutionaries and members of the National Society, approached Garibaldi. They asked him to lead a revolution in Palermo. Garibaldi refused the offer, believing there was little chance that any revolt in Sicily could succeed. The Neapolitan Army maintained a large garrison on the island, and all previous attempts at revolution had been brutally suppressed. Crispi continued to petition the revolutionary, finally convincing him.

For the next few months, Crispi and Garibaldi's lieutenants who had served with him in the Cacciatori delle Alpi and in Rome began to solicit volunteers for the expedition. Garibaldi and his officers recruited among the former Cacciatori and in Piedmontese regiments. The incredible success of the recruitment campaign gave Cavour pause, as hundreds of soldiers were leaving their regiments and volunteering. Cavour halted this practice to avoid weakening the Army in case of a renewed war with Austria. By May 1860, Garibaldi had assembled 1,089 men to participate in his adventure. It is here that the histories of the origin and course of the Sicilian expedition tend to generalize events, and the attitude of Cavour toward Garibaldi's plans. Cavour did not oppose Garibaldi's expedition, and in fact clandestinely supported it. His greatest concern was that a direct link between Piedmont–Sardinia and Garibaldi's expedition would be perceived by the European powers, and that they would seek to undermine both the campaign and Piedmont's bid for supremacy in Italy.

Before embarking on this adventure, Garibaldi once again pledged his loyalty to Victor Emmanuel II and proclaimed that his intention was to conquer Sicily for the king. Cavour tried desperately to separate Garibaldi's actions from Piedmontese policy, and this included using his influence to prevent the National Society from providing Garibaldi's troops with modern rifled muskets. Eminent historian Denis Mack Smith argued that Cavour's actions reflected his worry that Garibaldi was still a Mazzinian

radical at heart. Certainly, some of the volunteers were Mazzinians, but the events during and after Garibaldi's departure and arrival in Sicily indicate otherwise.

Garibaldi's forces assembled in Genoa in April. They were organized, equipped, and drilled prior to departing. Garibaldi acquired the use of two steamers, *Lombardo* and *Piemonte*. In the general discussion of Cavour's response to the expedition, the prime minister directed Admiral Persano, stationed at Sardinia, to intercept Garibaldi's expedition en route. Persano failed to locate Garibaldi, who made for the Papal coast first, before heading to Sicily. Nonetheless, if Cavour had desired to stop Garibaldi from departing, he need not have gone to the trouble of directing the Piedmontese fleet from Sardinia. Genoa was the main Piedmontese port city. Piedmontese troops, if not the naval commander of the port of Genoa, could have easily prevented *Piemonte* and *Lombardo* from departing. Cavour merely wanted to give the impression that the Piedmontese government did not sanction Garibaldi's actions.

There is every indication that there was far more collusion between Cavour and Garibaldi, if not Victor Emmanuel and Garibaldi. After Garibaldi landed in Sicily, Admiral Persano received orders to support the expedition. The rifles originally intended for the campaign arrived after Garibaldi took Palermo at the end of May. Lastly, throughout June and July 1860, Garibaldi's lieutenants led a stream of reinforcements from Genoa. More than 17,000 men had arrived in Sicily by August. Their recruitment and transport were quite conspicuous.

I Mille (The Thousand)

Garibaldi's art of warfare rested upon misdirection. His early campaigns in South America (1835–47), his defense of and retreat from Rome (1849), and the actions of the Cacciatori delle Alpi (1859) all bear the hallmarks of war of maneuver and surprise. News of Garibaldi's activities had reached Naples. The island garrison numbered 21,000 men divided between Siracusa and Messina,

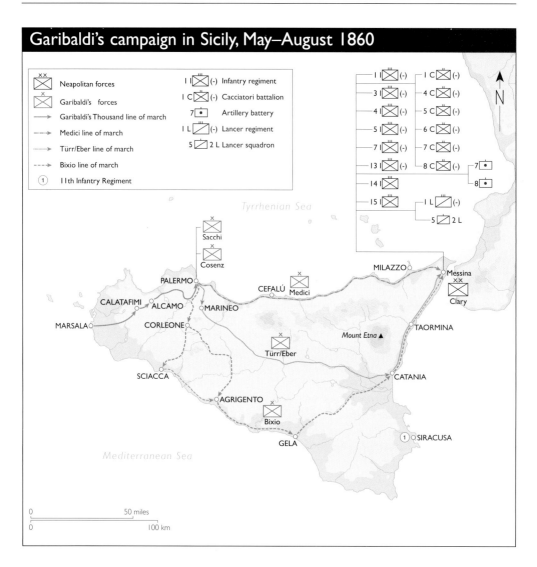

Garibaldi's campaign in Sicily, May–August 1860

Garibaldi landed on the island of Sicily with 1,089 men. After defeating the Neapolitans at Calatafimi, he stormed Palermo. Reinforcements from Piedmont raised his strength to more than 18,000 men during the month of July 1860. He directed his lieutenants to march in three columns across the island where he eliminated Bourbon rule in favor of his dictatorship.

but was increased to 40,000 after Garibaldi's expedition departed Genoa. The Neapolitan Navy was placed on alert and directed to intercept Garibaldi's ships. Garibaldi, however, struck first in central Italy, landing in Tuscany at Talamone. The raid was a diversion. From Tuscany, Garibaldi's ships headed toward Sicily. His objective was Palermo, but again Garibaldi eschewed the direct approach. Guided by Sicilian revolutionary Rosalino Pilo, the expedition sailed to the western tip of Sicily. Two Neapolitan warships spotted *Piemonte* and *Lombardo*. Garibaldi narrowly avoided them, and landed his volunteers under naval gunfire at Marsala on May 11. During the landing, and later at Palermo, Garibaldi benefited from the intervention of the British Royal Navy. Admiral Mundy was second in command of the Mediterranean fleet, and led the squadron off Palermo. Garibaldi had enormous popular support in England, and this translated into the actions of Mundy and his captains, who tried to provide cover for Garibaldi from the Neapolitan Navy. The Neapolitans were extremely cautious in dealing with their British counterparts and uniformly accepted British requests for parlay, which often worked to Garibaldi's advantage.

Once safely in Marsala, Garibaldi spent the next two days reorganizing his forces and gathering supplies. Giuseppe La Masa and Rosalino Pilo moved inland and began to raise units of *squadre*. These were Sicilian peasants who were enamored of Garibaldi, and desired to participate in the new revolution. Garibaldi's forces were organized into eight companies, including an elite company of Genoese Carabinieri, several cannon, and a staff. The majority of the Thousand had some sort of military experience. A substantial number had served in the Cacciatori the year before, but others were doctors, lawyers, shopkeepers, and students. They represented virtually all parts of Italy, though the most came from Lombardy, Venetia, and Piedmont. His officer corps too, represented the diverse regions of Italy, and included veterans such as Nino Bixio, Giuseppe Sirtori, Enrico Cosenz, and Stefan Türr. Giacomo Medici, one of Garibaldi's stalwart lieutenants, remained in Genoa to organize reinforcements. He accompanied the second expedition in June.

Lieutenant General Paolo Ruffo di Castelcicala, commander of Neapolitan forces in Palermo, received word of Garibaldi's landing. He dispatched two flying columns to intercept the Thousand. General Landi moved to the west, while Colonel Mechel headed south. Although Garibaldi's original position at Marsala was known, his subsequent movement remained a mystery. Garibaldi's objective was Palermo. The city had to be taken if the revolution in Sicily was to have any chance of success. He took the direct route to Palermo via Salemi and unexpectedly encountered Landi's column at Calatafimi on May 15.

The battle of Calatafimi, May 15, 1860

The battle of Calatafimi was the first of two critical engagements that were to decide the fate of Sicily. If Garibaldi was defeated at Calatafimi, he would lose the support of the

The landing of 'The Thousand' at Marsala, May 11, 1860. *Piemonte* and *Lombardo*, foreground, lie under the friendly guns of the British warships *Intrepid* and *Argus*. (Anne S.K. Brown Military Collection, Brown University Library)

peasants who had flocked to his banner in the previous week. Victory would open the road to Palermo. La Masa had gone into the hills to raise the *squadre* and by May 15 more than 700 had joined the Thousand. Garibaldi reorganized his companies into two battalions, one under Bixio, the other led by Colonel Carini. The battalions were deployed in two lines on Monte Pietralunga, with Carini's companies in front and Bixio in support. Garibaldi's three cannon were on his left and hundreds of *squadre*, on both flanks.

The Neapolitans deployed on the Piante dei Romani, across the valley from Garibaldi's forces. The hill was terraced, and offered solid ground on which to fight. The position forced the Garibaldini to move uphill against superior numbers. Landi led three battalions of infantry: the 8th Cacciatori, 2/10th Infantry, and 2nd Carabinieri. He had a squadron of light horse and four cannon; all totaled, 2,700 men. Garibaldi had 2,000, including the *squadre*. The latter, however, would offer no support in the actual fight, and served only to threaten the Neapolitan flanks.

The battle opened at 1.30pm. Landi chose his terrain well and Garibaldi had no choice but to direct a frontal assault uphill. Garibaldi ordered his lead companies not to offer fire, but to close with the bayonet. He understood that the position favored the defensive, and any delay in reaching the

The second decisive engagement in Sicily involved the storming of Palermo by Garibaldi and his troops. Volunteers and thousands of Sicilians fought the larger Neapolitan garrison in the streets for several days. Outgunned, Garibaldi and his supporters would have lost, but for the intervention of the commander of the British Mediterranean squadron Admiral Mundy. (The Art Archive/Museo del Risorgimento Brescia/Gianni Dagli Orti)

Neapolitan line would only give his enemy the advantage. The Neapolitan volleys were disciplined, and forced the first Garibaldinian companies to ground. Bixio's battalion came up on Carini's right, extending the line. Garibaldi drove his men forward. They took cover, and moved toward the Neapolitans in the intervals between firing. The fighting raged for almost three hours, when Landi's battalions ran out of ammunition. Realizing this, Garibaldi directed his men to the crest. Landi ordered a retreat as his troops began to waver. By 4pm Garibaldi commanded the Piante dei Romani. The victory cost Garibaldi 180 killed and wounded. Bourbon casualties were roughly equal.

Palermo

Success at Calatafimi emboldened Garibaldi to renew his advance on Palermo on May 17.

He followed the same route taken by Landi, but upon reaching Partinico he turned east. Garibaldi followed a circuitous route through the mountains, feinting north with *squadre* on May 21–22 and again on May 24. He then continued east and made his approach on Palermo from the southeast on May 27. The ten-day march confounded General Lanza, who had recently replaced Castelcicala. He dispatched Colonel Mechel from the city, but the Neapolitans were unable to locate Garibaldi's column and headed south toward Corleone, unaware that Garibaldi had skirted north. In the meantime, Garibaldi sent La Masa and Gilbrossa, who commanded the Sicilian peasant volunteers, into Palermo to organize resistance. When Garibaldi stormed the Porto Termini on May 27 he had 3,300 men including 750 of the Thousand.

The Garibaldini broke into Palermo and raised the city in revolution. In the weeks prior to the attack, Lanza had received reinforcements. He had 21,000 troops in the city and a squadron of warships in the harbor. Barricades were thrown up in the streets and fighting between Neapolitan troops and insurgents raged for two days. Neapolitan warships bombarded sections of the city, and it appeared as if Garibaldi's *coup de main* had failed. On May 30, Garibaldi's forces were running low on ammunition. To his good fortune disaster was averted by the intercession of British Admiral Mundy. His squadron lay off Palermo, observing the combat. He offered to negotiate between the two parties and bring calm to the city. Lanza feared that if he refused, Mundy's squadron would act to protect British citizens. Unknown to Lanza, Mundy had no such orders. The general therefore agreed to mediation, which concluded with an armistice until further direction was received from Naples. Lanza sailed to Naples where King Francis II authorized him to withdraw from Palermo. On July 7 the Neapolitan garrison boarded ships and sailed for Naples. Garibaldi would have failed without Mundy's intervention.

The fall of Palermo was the second critical event in Garibaldi's campaign in Sicily. His ability to seize the major commercial and population center of the island was a decisive victory. On the day of Lanza's departure, Garibaldi proclaimed himself Dictator of Sicily, "in the name of Victor Emmanuel, King of Italy," established a ministry of state, and decreed the creation of a National Guard. Two days earlier he had welcomed Giuseppe La Farina from the National Society who was dispatched as Cavour's personal representative. La Farina arrived in Palermo with the Piedmontese squadron under Admiral Persano.

Giacomo Medici arrived in Palermo with reinforcements within days of the victory. He commanded 3,500 volunteers and brought 8,000 rifled carbines and 400,000 rounds of ammunition. Garibaldi distributed these new weapons and ammunition, combined the new arrivals with the remnants of the Thousand, and renamed his forces the Southern Army. At the beginning of July, Garibaldi divided his army into three divisions, the 15th Division under General Stefan Türr, the 16th under Enrico Cosenz, and the 17th under Nino Bixio. Medici marched along the northern shore toward Messina, Cosenz advanced along the central route to Catania, and Bixio moved south and then along the coast toward Siracusa.

Rebel barricades in the streets of Palermo. (Alinari via Getty Images)

Francis II redistributed his army and reinforced the Neapolitan garrisons at Messina and Siracusa on the eastern shore. Revolution became the king's greatest concern, and overrode the fact that he still possessed military superiority in Sicily through the end of July. By ordering his forces to remain in and around these cities, he left the rest of the island to Garibaldi. This gave the new dictator the opportunity to extend his control over the island and gather more volunteers. Sicilians joined his ranks as the columns moved through the island. Moreover, thousands of reinforcements arrived during the month of July bringing the number of regular troops to more than 17,000 men. His Sicilian irregulars numbered perhaps 20,000 men.

The battle of Milazzo, July 19, 1860

Garibaldi controlled the road to Messina, but Marshal Clary, the newly appointed Bourbon commander in Sicily, did not remain passive. Prior to the arrival of Medici's column, Clary had dispatched Colonel Bosco to Milazzo, a fortress west of Messina that jutted out on a small peninsula into the Mediterranean. Milazzo was less than five miles from the road to Messina, and a Neapolitan garrison

Garibaldi attacked Neapolitan forces under Colonel Bosco at Milazzo, a fortress west of Messina. Garibaldi suffered heavy casualties and failed to defeat Bosco. The Neapolitans withdrew into the castle, and later took ship to Messina. (Anne S.K. Brown Military Collection, Brown University Library)

in the fortress could properly threaten communications between Palermo and Messina. Indeed, Garibaldi wanted to effect a crossing from the Straits of Messina to the mainland once he controlled Sicily. Leaving the enemy in Milazzo was not an option.

Colonel Bosco took advantage of his numbers and carried out several sorties against Medici's advanced posts observing the town and fortress. Bosco commanded 4,500 infantry and cavalry in Milazzo, and Medici had no more than 2,500 under his immediate command. The aggressiveness of the Neapolitans meant that Garibaldi had to turn his attention to this threat. He ordered Cosenz to Milazzo, giving Garibaldi slightly more than 4,000 men. On July 20, he attacked.

The battle of Milazzo was fought in two stages, the contest between Bosco and Garibaldi outside the fortress, and then the attack on the citadel. The fighting began in

the early morning hours. The even numbers and the professionalism of both forces led to heavy casualties and indecisive results. Bosco, however, could not afford to lose most of his men in a battle of attrition and withdrew later in the day behind the castle walls. Garibaldi had suffered some 750 casualties, more than 20 percent of his force. Bosco lost 200 men. The following day Garibaldi's warship *Türkory* arrived and bombarded the fortress. Shortly thereafter, Admiral Persano and the Piedmontese squadron appeared with orders to assist Garibaldi. To avoid annihilation, Bosco agreed to surrender his position with the honors of war. On August 1 he left Milazzo and was taken by ship to Messina, where he entered the citadel, still held by Clary.

Garibaldi was master of Sicily. The Neapolitans held nothing but the fortress in Messina, which was promptly placed under siege. Garibaldi commanded an army of more than 40,000 men, regulars and Sicilian volunteers. The Southern Army was considered by Garibaldi and Victor Emmanuel to be part of the Piedmontese Army. Over the next three weeks the Dictator of Sicily prepared to cross the Straits of Messina and march on Naples.

The conquest of Italy: Naples and the Papal States, August 1860–February 1861

Garibaldi's victory in Sicily was assured after the fall of Palermo, but his campaign on the mainland was far from certain. Although Cavour had secretly supported Garibaldi's expedition, he was quite wary of the strong Mazzinian elements among his officers and men. Garibaldi did not appreciate Cavour sending "spies" to the island to keep watch over him. Giuseppe La Farina was deported from Sicily at the end of July for sticking his nose into Garibaldi's affairs. Cavour was furious but did not stop the flow of men and material from Genoa. Perhaps the greatest concern to Cavour and King Victor Emmanuel was Garibaldi's intention to land in Naples and march on the capital. That alone was not so terrible, but Garibaldi had also stated his intention to march on Rome.

During the course of Cavour's hiatus as prime minister between July 10, 1859 and his return to office on January 20, 1860, Piedmontese relations with the papacy declined steadily. Victor Emmanuel played upon Napoleon III's guilty conscience and gained the French emperor's support for the eventual annexation of the Papal Romagna and Legations. Napoleon III, however, demanded guarantees that Pius IX would be safe in Rome, with Umbria and the Marche still under papal rule. Garibaldi's intentions in August threatened this understanding and could lead to French and Austrian actions; or at least this was the excuse given to Napoleon III after the Piedmontese Army invaded the Papal States in September 1860.

The timing of Garibaldi's crossing of the Straits of Messina and the invasion of the Papal States was more than coincidence. Garibaldi's first troops disembarked during the third week of August and began a methodical advance toward Naples. At the same time, General Enrico Cialdini met with Napoleon III in Savoy to press the claim that military intervention in the Papal States was necessary to preserve the general peace. The French emperor too played it to the hilt, believing Cavour in so far as he could use this excuse as cover against French Catholic opposition. Neither Cavour nor Napoleon III was completely sincere. Each believed that he was manipulating the other.

On September 6 King Francis II fled Naples for the fortress city of Gaeta. His navy's failure to prevent the landing compounded his fear of revolution. The king moved his army to the Volturno River, and waited. Garibaldi and his troops entered the city and raised local forces before marching north. On September 11 the Piedmontese Army crossed the Papal frontier, inaugurating the final campaign of the Second War of Italian Unification. To all in Italy and throughout Europe these events meant collusion.

Conquest of the Papal States

A Piedmontese army was deployed in Tuscany and the former Papal Legations. Orders were coded, unlike 1859, and troops concentrated with the utmost secrecy. The invasion force under General Manfredo Fanti included two corps, IV and V, led by Cialdini and Enrico Della Rocca respectively, and comprised 40,000 infantry and cavalry and 78 guns. This was more than sufficient to contend with the Papal Army under General Lamoricière. The former French general had accepted his position as head of the Papal Army at the beginning of the year and had spent the previous nine months recruiting and reorganizing the army. More than 20,000 men filled the ranks, drawn from domestic and international recruitment.

Lamoricière understood that any war with Piedmont could not be won without allies, and expected that both Napoleon III and Franz Josef would send relief armies to the pope's aid. His strategy was to delay the Piedmontese invasion long enough for these expeditionary corps to arrive. With Rome and Civitavecchia under French garrison since 1849, Lamoricière had to hold Ancona on the Adriatic in anticipation of an Austrian landing. Unfortunately for Pius IX, no help was forthcoming. Lamoricière had 13,000 men available for field duty, divided into four brigades. The remainder were employed in garrisons throughout Umbria and the Marche.

Cavour justified the invasion of the Papal States when revolutionaries raised their banners – at Cavour's instigation – and attacked Papal gendarmes and Guardia di Finanza in several towns. The response by Papal regulars was used as the *casus belli*. King Victor Emmanuel II could not stand idly by while fellow Italians were being slaughtered. Thus, on September 11, Cialdini's IV Corps crossed the border and attacked Papal troops in Pesaro. The town guarded the coastal road toward Ancona. To the west in the Apennines, Della Rocca's V Corps headed for Perugia via Città di Castello.

Papal forces were highly dedicated to defending the temporal lands of Pius IX, but they were woefully outnumbered. At Pesaro and Città di Castello the small garrisons made a stalwart defense, but Piedmontese artillery wreaked havoc with the medieval gates and walls of the castles. Only a few cities in the Papal domain had proper 19th-century fortifications. Thus, the defenses crumbled and troop morale plunged. Officers were forced by circumstance and their own men to ask for terms. Two days after the invasion, Perugia and Ancona were threatened.

Lamoricière rushed toward Ancona, leaving one brigade under General Schmidt to defend Perugia. Ancona had to be held, as it was the only port on the Adriatic that could accommodate an Austrian fleet and expeditionary corps. The Papal commander-in-chief did not count on either the speed of the Piedmontese advance, or the commitment of the Piedmontese Navy to blockading Ancona. Even so, no Austrian assistance was forthcoming. Lamoricière determined to reach Ancona before Cialdini arrived. It is unclear if Lamoricière wanted to force a battle outside the walls, or simply reinforce the garrison before the city was placed under siege.

The Papal Army marched on Ancona via Macerata on September 13. Lamoricière's columns moved through Spoleto and Fogliano only hours before the leading Bersaglieri battalions from V Corps came down the same road in the opposite direction. From Macerata the Papal Army took secondary roads to the coast and then north toward Ancona. Cialdini, however, had been informed of Lamoricière's movement. He deployed the 4th Division on the heights above the Musone River near the town of Castelfidardo. When Lamoricière arrived at Loreto on September 17, he spied the Piedmontese position. Undeterred, he planned to cross the Musone, screen the Piedmontese regiments with a column under General Pimodan, and slide the rest of the army across the river and toward Ancona.

The battle of Castelfidardo on September 18 was the largest engagement between Piedmontese and Papal forces in 1860. Pimodan's battalions forded the Musone and moved uphill against the Piedmontese position. Cialdini had 8,000 men and three batteries in the area, but only the 26th Bersaglieri Battalion and 10th Infantry Regiment in the immediate vicinity. Pimodan moved his troops to the north bank with skill, but the Bersaglieri delayed their advance until reinforcements arrived. The second column began to cross the Musone. With Pimodan severely wounded, Lamoricière took over the combat. Distracted by the event unfolding to their front, and with regiments from the Piedmontese 4th Division arriving, the Papal Army moved back across the Musone, while only a few battalions made it past the fighting at Castelfidardo. Lamoricière moved north along the road to Ancona as Piedmontese infantry pursued. Those troops at Loreto surrendered. The Papal commander arrived in Ancona that night with a paltry force. Over the next several days Cialdini's men continued to isolate and capture the remnants of Lamoricière's army. By the third week of September it had ceased to exist.

The siege of Ancona began on September 18, the same day as the battle at Castelfidardo. Admiral Persano, commanding the Piedmontese squadron in the Adriatic, opened a bombardment of the city. Persano's fleet transported the siege train, thereby quickly providing Cialdini with proper equipment to progress the siege. The combined naval and land bombardments were devastatingly effective. Fanti wanted the city to fall as quickly as possible, and diverted most of Della Rocca's V Corps to support Cialdini. After ten days several outer works were taken, and the gates of the city were threatened by assault. Naval gunfire rained on the citadel, and Lamoricière had little choice but to surrender the city on September 29.

The fall of Ancona ended the campaign in the Papal States. The Piedmontese Army occupied most of Umbria and the Marche. Two days later Garibaldi narrowly defeated the Neapolitan Army on the Volturno. The concern that he intended immediately to march on Rome dissipated. This was a meager consolation prize for Pius IX, who now ruled merely the city of Rome and its environs; the territories that had been Papal domain for over 1,000 years were soon to become part of the new Kingdom of Italy.

The battle of the Volturno, October 1, 1860

The Army of the Kingdom of the Two Sicilies was divided among the large garrisons of Gaeta, Capua, and Messina and the field army of 25,000 men. The Neapolitan Army held a strong position on the Volturno. Two infantry and one cavalry division camped outside Capua, with a third infantry division spread upstream holding the fords and bridges across the river. Garibaldi's army had advanced to positions from Santa Maria to Caserta and Maddaloni a week earlier. His army now boasted 22,000 men divided among four divisions. Most of these men

The battle of the Volturno, October 3, 1860, was fought between the Southern Army under Garibaldi, and the Neapolitan forces defending Capua. The Neapolitans wanted to conduct a double envelopment of Garibaldi's army, but poor coordination allowed Garibaldi to repel the piecemeal attacks. This Dublin woodcut celebrates the role of the Irish Brigade in Neapolitan service. (Anne S.K. Brown Military Collection, Brown University Library)

The siege of Gaeta, November 1860–February 1861

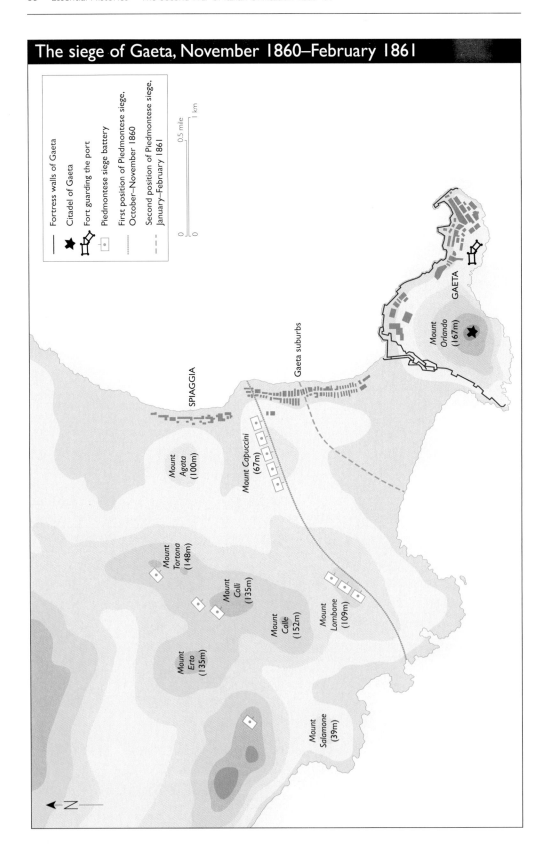

Fortress walls of Gaeta

Citadel of Gaeta

Fort guarding the port

Piedmontese siege battery

First position of Piedmontese siege, October–November 1860

Second position of Piedmontese siege, January–February 1861

0.5 mile   1 km

GAETA

Mount Orlando (167m)

Gaeta suburbs

SPIAGGIA

Mount Agata (100m)

Mount Capuccini (67m)

Mount Tortona (148m)

Mount Colli (135m)

Mount Colle (152m)

Mount Lombone (109m)

Mount Erto (135m)

Mount Salamone (39m)

N

Opposite: the fortress city of Gaeta had been a haven for Neapolitan kings. Its location at the tip of a peninsula made it ideal for defense. King Francis II withdrew to Gaeta after Garibaldi landed in southern Italy. The remnants of his army took refuge in the city, which was promptly placed under siege by the Piedmontese from November 1860 through February 1861. The surrender of Gaeta paved the way for unification of northern and southern Italy the following month.

had served in Sicily, now supplemented by more volunteers.

Garibaldi despised positional warfare. The skirmishing between the armies had agitated the general. He determined to pin the Neapolitan Army under the walls of Capua, while crossing the Volturno and cutting off the king at Gaeta from his army. Simultaneously, the Neapolitan generals concurred that Garibaldi had placed his army in a precarious position between the divisions at Capua and the brigades of Mechel and Ruiz at Dugenta. They saw an opportunity to destroy Garibaldi's forces by

conducting a double-envelopment of the Southern Army.

On October 1 the armies moved in chorus. The Neapolitans struck first. Before 6am, General Anfan de Rivera's division attacked Giacomo Medici's 17th Division at Sant'Angelo. To the south, General Tabacchi's and General Ruggeri's divisions advanced on the 16th Division under General Milbiz at Santa Maria. Mechel's brigade pushed in the lead battalions of Bixio's 18th Division northeast of Maddaloni.

From Caserta Garibaldi was able to dispense the reserve to either flank. Garibaldi

The defenses of the fortified city of Gaeta were formidable. The fortifications extended beyond the citadel, with a peninsula protected by walls preventing any attempt at a *coup de main*. The city was bombarded by the Piedmontese by sea and land until February 1861 when King Francis II surrendered. Here, on February 5, 1861, a Piedmontese shell penetrates a powder magazine, causing a massive explosion. A French ship six miles away reportedly felt the blast. (De Agostini/Getty Images)

properly assessed the threat to his left, and moved reinforcements to support Milbiz and Medici. He went to Santa Maria in person, leaving Türr with the 15th Division at Caserta. On the right, some of Mechel's battalions lost their way during their march on Maddaloni. This allowed Bixio to concentrate his forces and repel the initial attacks. Fighting raged throughout the day, but by 2pm Medici and Milbiz had determined that the Neapolitans were spent, and issued a counterattack. The renewed vigor of the Garibaldini forced the Neapolitans back to Capua. The success came just in time, as Ruiz's brigade moved directly upon Caserta. Türr held the town until Medici sent aid. On the far right, Mechel's uncoordinated attacks stalled, and he withdrew by the late afternoon.

Garibaldi narrowly won the battle of Volturno. He lost 2,000 killed, wounded, and prisoner, while the Neapolitans suffered 3,000 casualties and prisoners. The day after the battle, the Savoia Brigade of the Piedmontese army landed by sea north of Capua. Over the next several weeks Della Rocca's V Corps crossed the Neapolitan frontier, followed by the rest of the Piedmontese Army. The Southern Army placed Capua under siege, and Piedmontese forces marched on Gaeta where the erstwhile Neapolitan king had taken refuge.

Gaeta

During the weeks following Garibaldi's victory on the Volturno, Piedmontese columns moved south to join with the Southern Army. The scant Neapolitan forces in the interior offered resistance, but merely delayed the advance of the Piedmontese Army. Della Rocca's V Corps arrived at Caserta and Capua toward the end of the month. On October 26 King Victor Emmanuel II met Garibaldi at Teano, east of Caserta. Garibaldi had decided shortly after the Volturno to hand command of the Southern Army to the Piedmontese. His meeting with the king marked the end of his role in the Second War of Italian Unification. Although disappointed that Rome and Venetia remained outside the new kingdom, he retired to his home on the island of Caprera.

Cialdini's IV Corps operated to the north. The fortress city of Gaeta posed a particularly difficult problem. Located on a peninsula, and supported by the Neapolitan Navy, Gaeta could only be attacked from one side. The garrison consisted of 12,000 men, and proper artillery. In 1806, the city had held out for months against a French army under Marshal André Masséna. Even with the arrival of the Piedmontese squadron, the siege would take much longer than at Ancona. The fortress was invested on November 12.

The siege of Gaeta lasted 100 days. Francis II surrendered the city on February 14, 1861. More than 55,000 rounds were fired against the defenses. The fall of the city meant the end of the Kingdom of the Two Sicilies and victory for the House of Savoy. The isolated garrisons at Messina and Civitavella del Tronto surrendered the following month, but their defiance did not prevent Victor Emmanuel from assuming the crown of Italy. On March 17 the Parliament proclaimed the King of Piedmont–Sardinia as Victor Emmanuel I, King of Italy.

Giuseppe Cesare Abba and Garibaldi's Thousand

Giuseppe Cesare Abba was one of the most prolific authors of Garibaldi's Thousand. At the age of 22, Abba was an aspiring poet and writer. He heeded the call to arms in 1860 and joined Garibaldi's expedition. Desiring to recount his exploits for posterity he kept a diary, taking careful notes of events, his comrades, and the experience of war. His observations provide an unambiguous, and often romantic recollection of the campaign in Sicily and Naples, but Abba did not alter the record later, leaving his diary as one of the best first-hand accounts of the Thousand.

Abba produced a Homeric epic of his experience, *Da Quarto al Volturno* (From Quarto to Volturno) in 1866, only a few years after his adventure. He published his diary, *Noterelle d'uno dei Mille: edite dopo vent'anni* (Notes of one of the Mille: edited after twenty years), in 1880. It was an immediate success and brought Abba fame. Thereafter he penned a larger account of the Thousand, *Storia dei Mille* (1904) and in the following year a wonderfully lively biography of his former commander, *Vita di Nino Bixio* (1905). In addition to his historical observations, Abba continued to write poetry and the occasional novel.

Abba hailed from Parma, which had only recently voted for annexation to Piedmont. "Poor Duke! [of Parma]," he wrote, "King Victor takes possession of your Duchy. The latter is certainly fortunate! Anyone who wishes to do something for Italy, even if no friend of kings must be prepared to add to his glory …" Although a constitutionalist, he was no Mazzinian. Like many young men, Abba was a Garibaldino and perfectly happy to accept a unified Italy that had a constitution and a king.

The diary provides insight into the method of recruitment and the composition of the Thousand. Recruitment of volunteers was conducted directly by Garibaldi's lieutenants among the ranks of the Piedmontese Army and by word of mouth. Romagnoles and Piedmontese joined Abba and his acquaintances en route to Genoa. All traveled to the port city, having been inspired by rumors. On May 3, from Novi, Abba wrote:

Well, our party is growing larger and better. On the platform there are some infantry soldiers waiting for a train. A second lieutenant comes over to me and says: "Would you send me a wire from Genoa telling me when you are to sail?" I hesitated and didn't answer. What was I to say after our security warning? The officer looked at me in the eyes and understood. "Ah well," he said smiling, "keep your secret, but believe me I have no bad intentions in asking." [2]

Operational security was of paramount importance. It is clear that Garibaldi's intentions were an open secret, but the specifics remained unknown.

Abba boarded *Lombardo* on May 5, having not yet spied Garibaldi. The general was on *Piemonte* and Nino Bixio commanded the other ship. Abba first saw Garibaldi a day after the landing at Marsala: "A smile on his face, radiating confidence, Garibaldi, with his General Staff, brought up the rear. He rode a bay horse fit for a Vizier. The saddle was magnificent, the stirrups decorated with filigree work. He wore a red shirt and grey trousers, with a Hungarian-style hat on his head and a silk handkerchief round his neck …" A short while later Abba again observed Garibaldi during a short rest: "The General,

---

2 This and the following extracts are taken from Giuseppe Cesare Abba, *The Diary of One of Garibaldi's Thousand*, translated by E. R. Vincent (London: Oxford University Press, 1962)

Giuseppe Garibaldi pictured in a newspaper with "two of his favorite volunteers" from the Thousand. This is an engraving after Pagliano, an artist and Risorgimento activist who fought in the 1848 revolt in Milan, and under Garibaldi at Varese in 1859. (Anne S.K. Brown Military Collection, Brown University Library)

seated at the foot of an olive tree, eats his bread and cheese, slicing it with his own knife and chatting simply with those around. I look at him and have a feeling of the greatness of bygone days."

Garibaldi's legend had enabled him to recruit his volunteers on relatively short notice. They sailed, marched, and followed. Abba's account of the battle of Calatafimi is written with the sincerity and shock of his first experience of combat. He lost his friend Sartori on the terraces of the Piante dei Romani, and witnessed bravery and death.

The first, second and third terraces up the hillside were attacked at the point of a bayonet and passed, but it was terrible to see the dead and wounded. Little by little, as they yielded ground, the Royalist [Neapolitan] battalions retreated higher up. They concentrated and thus grew stronger. At last it seemed impossible that we could face them. They were all on top of the hill and we were around the brow, tired, at the

end of our tether, and reduced in numbers. There was a moment of pause; it was difficult to recognize the two opposing sides, they up there and we all flat on the ground. One could hear the rifle fire and the Royalist troops started rolling down boulders, and hurling stones …

It was at this point in the battle that Garibaldi realized that the Neapolitan troops were running out of ammunition, hence throwing stones. Not long after, the order for the final charge to the crest was given and a *mêlée* ensued. Abba survived the battle physically unscathed, but his comments concerning the carnage and the death of his friend provide an honest accounting of his feelings that night as he reflected on the events of the day.

"Hell or Palermo," shouted Bixio to his men after their long march through the mountains around Palermo. Abba recalled the various Sicilian villages, the peasants, and the *picciotti*, those young men who joined the ranks following the Garibaldini to Palermo. Abba's account of the fighting in Palermo is as dramatic as his description of Calatafimi. The combat in the streets, the dead and wounded women, and the bombardment from the citadel Castellamare are all prominently recorded.

The Royalists have done things fit for savages. Towards eleven that day Magarita and I, in an alley, found the corpse of a fifteen-year-old girl. She was beautiful even in death, and never have I been so moved as by the sight of that corpse. She had been violated and her tender body wounded in many parts until a bayonet thrust through the neck must have freed her from her torments.

The fear and rumors of Neapolitan reinforcements, and the foreign navies in the harbor, added to the uncertainty of the outcome of the battle for the city. Abba and his comrades were relieved by the armistice and thrilled when the Neapolitans abandoned the city weeks later. The Thousand remained at Palermo, recovering from the difficult fight and counting their wounds.

The street fighting in Palermo involved the use of artillery, and the deliberate bombardment of sections of the city from the citadel. Neapolitan warships joined in with the shelling. The destruction was limited to a few parts of town, but the impact was devastating. Shown here are the ruins of Palazzo Carini. (Alinari via Getty Images)

Abba's vivid account also provides answers to some questions concerning the collusion between Cavour and Garibaldi. On June 21 Abba wrote that Giacomo Medici arrived, "with a regiment already organized and equipped ... The vanguard was composed of forty officers in the uniform of the Piedmontese Army." He continued:

We of the original expedition are lost in the flood of newcomers, but treasure the memory of the twenty-five days when we toiled and fought in faith alone. Now we are to go through the island, recruiting men and passing like pilgrims from place to place, until the enemy stops us and we come to blows and blood once more or unite for the honor of Italy.

Abba recorded the march across the island, and the crossing of the Straits of Messina. He participated in the capture of Naples and the battle of the Volturno and remained with the remnant of the Thousand through the end of the war. Abba's company was incorporated into Stefan Türr's brigade after Palermo, and then the 15th Division of the Southern Army. He is one of the few who elucidate on the daily events of the expedition, and his contemporary notes establish the unmistakable relationship between Garibaldi and Victor Emmanuel, if not Cavour, in completing the final phase of the Second War of Italian Unification.

The threat of a general European war

The threat of a general European conflict in 1859 was very real, but Napoleon III worked well to prevent it. As much as Cavour pressed the French emperor through the spring, the prime minister did not control events. It is clear that without guarantees from Czar Alexander II, Napoleon would not have pursued the conflict. He benefited from Britain's desire to avoid the outbreak of hostilities, and used Britain's diplomatic initiatives to his advantage. It remains unclear what course the Italian crisis would have taken in April 1859, if Franz Josef had not issued the ultimatum.

In the years preceding the war, Franz Josef and his advisors and ministers inadvertently pursued policies that assured diplomatic isolation. Austria's attitude toward the German Confederation and Prussia resulted in animosity toward Vienna. As the President of the German Confederation, Franz Josef had specific responsibilities to protect the interests of the German states. Certainly, the Confederation as envisioned by Metternich at the Congress of Vienna had been a tool to reassert Habsburg power in Germany after the Napoleonic era. It succeeded for many decades, but by 1848–49 Prussia was a significant economic and political force. Industrialization and the establishment of the Zollverein, the German Customs Union, ensured Prussia's economic domination of the Confederation. Furthermore, Austria's gradual development of an industrial economy and Prussia's purposeful exclusion of its rival from the organization created tensions.

The German revolutions of 1848–49 posed an enormous threat to Austrian power. Representatives from the various states met at Frankfurt in 1848 to discuss the formal unification of Germany under a constitutional monarchy. The Prussian delegation to the Frankfurt Parliament included a young, staunch conservative, Otto von Bismarck. Conservatives like Bismarck rejected the notion that a parliament could offer an imperial crown to a monarch, but the liberals outnumbered and outvoted their colleagues. In 1849, the Frankfurt Parliament offered the crown of a united Germany to Frederick William IV, King of Prussia. He famously retorted, "I shall not accept a crown from the gutter."

The rebuff of the imperial crown was not an indication that the Prussian monarchy – the Hohenzollerns – did not desire to preside over Germany. They wanted it on their own terms. Franz Josef responded to these events with intimidation. If Prussia did not formally renounce interests in the German throne, Austria would go to war. In 1850, Frederick William IV traveled to Olmütz, where he acceded to Austrian demands. The Prussian monarch and nationalists did not soon forget the Peace of Olmütz, referred by the Prussians as the "humiliation of Olmütz."

Franz Josef continued to treat the German Confederation as his domain. When in 1857 a crisis over Neuchâtel demanded Austrian support of Confederation rights, Franz Josef refused to sanction imperial participation. This was seen as a slight to the Confederation and the interests of the states. Prussia, ever mindful of its role in the Confederation, continued to play upon Austria's alienating actions through active participation. Imperial hubris is perhaps the proper way to characterize Franz Josef's philosophy. He was born a century too late to conduct Habsburg policy in this manner.

Count Bernard Rechberg served as Franz Josef's ambassador to the Federal Diet of the German Confederation. He entered the Habsburg Foreign Service during Metternich's tenure. He held the former chancellor's confidence, particularly in German affairs. Rechberg was an ardent advocate of a *rapprochement* between Prussia and the Austrian Empire. He was therefore perfectly suited in 1859 to gain the support of the Confederation. Unfortunately, the Diet was ill disposed toward Austrian concerns about Piedmont, especially when Confederation territory was not immediately threatened. This was the Austrian argument in 1857 when they rejected Confederation demands for action in Switzerland.

Count Carl von Buol served as foreign minister of the Austrian Empire through May 1859. He mistakenly believed that Austria was in a stronger position in the international community than was truly the case. He did not fully appreciate the Russian enmity that remained after 1856. Moreover, he overestimated the extent to which Prince Wilhelm, who was the Prince Regent of Prussia between 1858 and 1861 after Frederick William suffered a stroke, was sympathetic toward Austria's predicament. Buol wrongly believed that the current situation surrounding the Prussian monarchy translated into weakness, or at least a lack of desire to upset the balance in Germany. This was far from the truth. Wilhelm was far more hawkish concerning Prussia's role in Germany than his brother. He surrounded himself with advisors, ministers, and generals who agreed with his staunch conservative-nationalist views.

By April 1859 Franz Josef's ambassadors in Berlin and Frankfurt had failed to provide definitive answers as to whether Austria could count on German support. Feldmarschall Hess and Count Grünne surprisingly agreed that if France joined the Piedmontese in Italy, "Lombardy depended on the Rhine." It is ironic that, in 1805, Napoleon I had advocated the same strategic philosophy when the Austrians prepared to invade French-held Lombardy.

Franz Josef sent his cousin, the Archduke Albrecht, as special envoy to Berlin on April 10. The Habsburg Prince was the son of the famed Austrian military leader, the Archduke Karl. Albrecht possessed a solid reputation

and substantial respect among the military administration. Like his father, Albrecht was a realist and had little taste for diplomacy. Prince Wilhelm made certain that Albrecht was properly entertained, but serious discussions were avoided. Upon his return to Vienna, Albrecht wrote the prince regent, expressing his appreciation for a pleasant visit, noting, "I am not a diplomat and am heartily glad to leave the slippery path of diplomacy ... I am quite content in my military sphere, and thank heaven only a soldier." Pleasantries aside, Albrecht understood all too well that his treatment in Berlin indicated that Prussia would not actively support Austria in the impending war. Nonetheless, Franz Josef, Buol, Rechberg, Hess, and Grünne clung to the belief that Prussia and the Confederation would ally with Austria.

Prussia's response to Austrian overtures throughout the first months of 1859 illustrated a royal administration seeking to redefine its position in Germany and Europe. Prince Wilhelm, his minister of war General Edward von Bonin, and his personal military advisor General Albrecht von Roon, saw the looming crisis as a means to advance Prussia's position in the Confederation at the expense of Austria, without committing Prussia to war. When they demanded that Prussia lead the Federal Army if war came, Austria refused. Feldmarschall Hess had previously served as commander of the Federal Army, and adamantly rejected the proposal. Franz Josef, too, gave it no consideration. If the Austrian emperor agreed, it would work to Prussia's advantage. By refusing, Prussia would watch developments from the sideline.

Much is made by historians about the role of Helmuth von Moltke, Chief of the Prussian General Staff in 1859. He despised Napoleon III and saw great opportunity to strike at France. Prince Wilhelm asked him to explore timetables in case of mobilization, but Moltke read this as the prince's desire to mobilize. Moltke reported in March that it would require several months to properly prepare the Army and deploy it on the Rhine. His estimates were shaded by his interest in

Kaiser Franz Josef and Emperor Napoleon III met on the morning of 11 July to agree on an armistice. Despite the French victory at Solferino, threat of a general European war led both emperors to accept peace. (Anne S.K. Brown Military Collection, Brown University Library)

convincing the Prince to begin preparations long before any conflict. Moltke misunderstood Wilhelm's curiosity. The prince was looking at options, but Moltke was the only one among the senior military leaders who wanted war with France.

At this time, the Chief of the Prussian General Staff had no influence on policy, and his role was relegated to war planning and management. The Moltke of 1859 did not have the same influence as in 1866 or 1870. Historians, and students of history, should not imagine that the "great" Moltke had any sort of influence on the prince, the court, and advisors. During the last week of April, Moltke told Wilhelm it would take three to four weeks to prepare seven of the eight corps necessary for a campaign. Transporting the

corps to the Rhine frontier would take additional time. The prince authorized the activation of three corps, but did not go as far as decreeing mobilization. When the prince finally gave the order to mobilize the Army in June, Moltke acted and the Prussian Army gradually moved into position along the Rhine. It was the second week of July when the Prussian corps were ready for operations. Unfortunately for Moltke, the Peace of Villafranca was signed, and the war over. Prussian mobilization therefore remained an exercise. It is possible that Moltke's vocal support for a war with France, heard indirectly by Rechberg and Buol in March, gave Franz Josef a false sense of Prussian intentions.

As much as Franz Josef desired to expand the war beyond Italy, Napoleon III sought to limit its scope. To this end Russia played a critical role. Napoleon III carried out secret negotiations with Czar Alexander II in the fall of 1858 after the Plombières agreement and through the formal Franco-Piedmontese convention of December. His foreign minister, Count Walewski, a cousin and the bastard son of Emperor Napoleon I, served as window-dressing to the imperial regime. Napoleon III did not conduct serious negotiations through his foreign minister. He relied upon his other cousin, Prince Jérôme Napoleon, and military attaché Le Roncière Le Noury to make official proposals. Napoleon III sought Russian neutrality in the coming conflict, and hoped that Czar Alexander II might consider deploying Russian troops on the Austrian frontier. An increased Russian military presence on Austria's border might prevent Franz Josef from reinforcing his army in Italy with troops from Galicia and Bohemia.

Since 1815, Russia had maintained an anti-Napoleonic, anti-French attitude, which had contributed to the outbreak of the Crimean War. Franz Josef's refusal to support Russia during the war, and his subsequent conduct to undermine Russia's influence in the Balkans was seen as betrayal. Otto von Bismarck, then Prussian ambassador to St Petersburg, reported a decided anti-Austrian mood in Russia. An agreement with France would alter the course that had been set for the past 40 years. Nevertheless this received uniform support from Prince Gorchakov, the Russian foreign minister. Russian interest in French proposals offered more than a chance at revenge against Austria. The czar and his foreign minister desired significant revisions to the Treaty of Paris (1856), which had officially concluded the Crimean War. Negotiations between Paris and St Petersburg focused upon modifications to the treaty. Alexander however made it very clear that he would only bring his corps in Poland to full strength, but would not break off relations with Austria, nor desire intervention of Prussia and the German Confederation. If a wider war occurred, Napoleon III could not count on Russia. Alexander agreed to posturing, but nothing more. Napoleon III accepted the terms and signed the treaty on March 3, 1859.

When war came Alexander held to his agreements. The Russian Army maintained its

Franz Josef (r. 1848–1916) became Emperor of Austria at the age of eighteen. The nephew of Emperor Ferdinand II, Franz Josef ascended the throne during the tempestuous time of the 1848 revolutions. He secured his throne through the support of his generals and remained wedded to the Habsburg Imperial Army. He assumed personal command of the army in Lombardy–Venetia shortly after the defeat of his army at Magenta in 1859. (Anne S.K. Brown Military Collection, Brown University Library)

position on the Galician frontier, but did nothing more. Prince Gorchakov sought to keep the rest of Europe out of the conflict. He maintained close ties with Bismarck, and Russian ambassadors in Germany. During the first month of the campaign everything held steady. When in June the Franco-Piedmontese army crossed the Ticino into Lombardy, thereby invading Austrian territory, the situation in the Federal Diet and Berlin began to change. Austria's invasion of Piedmont had nothing to do with the German Confederation, but the invasion of Lombardy had specific constitutional implications for Confederation members. They were required to come to Austria's aid.

Prince Gorchakov found it increasingly difficult to restrain Prussia through moderation. He was unaware that Wilhelm was posturing. Events in Germany were only one of several concerns that permeated

Alexander's court in June. Austria's military defeat appeared certain after Magenta and Solferino. While the decline of Austrian power was not an idea opposed in St Petersburg, it would be replaced with French power. Unlike Austria, France was a wealthy, industrial state that possessed a large army and a navy capable of exporting French power around the world. Russia's role as a neutral state served the immediate purpose of wounding an enemy for diplomatic gain, but Alexander did not seek the complete restructuring of the international system over the Italian question.

Britain's position regarding the events in Italy changed over the course of 1859–60. Initially, the Earl of Derby's government desired to prevent war through an international conference, and succeeded in gaining support during the spring from all parties. Lord Malmesbury, the foreign secretary, worked to calm tensions, much to Cavour's dismay. He would have succeeded, had Franz Josef not issued the ultimatum. A week after Magenta, Derby's government fell, and Lord Palmerston returned to office. His administration was quite sympathetic to the Italian question, although not terribly favorable toward Napoleon III. The Peace of Villafranca was seen as an act of moderation, as was the Treaty of Zurich, which officially ended the war.

Although Cavour was perceived as a rather wily fellow, Garibaldi had substantial support from the British prime minister and his cabinet. It is clear that during Garibaldi's expedition to Sicily, the role of Admiral Mundy was probably not directly sanctioned by Palmerston, but neither did Mundy receive rebuke for his actions, which directly resulted in Garibaldi's victory in Palermo. Subsequently, Garibaldi's conquest of Naples, and its union with Piedmont, meant a new state in the Mediterranean that was opposed to Austria and not in the French camp after Villafranca. There was significant opportunity for Britain to establish a firm relationship with the new Kingdom of Italy.

Britain had no interest in being drawn into the Second War of Italian Unification. It was already coping with the aftermath of the Indian Uprising and French plans for a canal at Suez. Tensions between Britain and China were equally raised and war loomed. Both Derby and Palmerston struggled to ensure the maintenance of a continental peace without risking direct British intervention. The turn of events in 1859 and 1860 worked in Britain's favor, though except for Mundy's role at Palermo, Britain remained aloof from the conflict.

Franz Josef gambled with the fate of Italy as Austria continued to balance its power between the German Confederation and Italian states while contending with growing domestic unrest and economic problems. The Austrian emperor and his advisors believed that the empire must look strong everywhere. Beyond this appearance of strength, Franz Josef and his advisors believed that Austria was strong; and it was. The weakness of the imperial regime was found not in the military but in the diplomatic sphere. A decade of neo-absolutism at home and an arrogant foreign policy served to alienate Austria's neighbors and former allies. This resulted in the loss of Habsburg power in Italy, save Venetia, and the growing rift with Prussia and Russia.

An anonymous Neapolitan account

There are many first-hand accounts of active participants of the Second War of Italian Unification, but only a few from civilians. The following chapter is drawn from an anonymous Neapolitan author, who was clearly sympathetic to revolution and ultimately a supporter of Garibaldi. The relation represents an edited and enhanced observation of Neapolitan society and politics from the death of Ferdinand II to the meeting of Garibaldi and Victor Emmanuel at Teano. The book was originally published in 1861, with a subsequent edition printed in 1867, the year of the battle of the Mentana.

As the war between Austria, France, and Piedmont commenced, the Neapolitan regime was dumbfounded when at the same time King Ferdinand II, known as "King Bomba," for his prodigious use of artillery against insurgents, fell ill.

May 1, 1859
There is a confusion of fears and hopes as the government remains suspended.

The effect is an uncertainty worse than war, and chaos worse than revolution.

There is a striking contrast between the events in northern and southern Italy.

Up there, the Piedmontese united with France, rely strongly on the undying ideas of patriotism and freedom; by all counts, King Ferdinand II, abandoned by his people and Europe, is the irreconcilable enemy of liberal ideas, and the concept of Italy.

The universal sympathy for Victor Emmanuel, and the indifference with which you look at the deathbed of Ferdinand, already illustrate the opinion of history.[3]

Ferdinand's death and the accession of his son Francis II gave some in Naples pause. The king pledged to institute reforms, but the people remained skeptical. The progress of the war in the north created a rather volatile atmosphere in which the police made arrests and prohibited demonstrations.

June 17, 1859
At the news of the victory of Magenta, a demonstration of over two thousand Neapolitans was held in support of France and Italy under the balcony of the French and Piedmontese consuls.

This demonstration was dispersed by bayonets, but the king remained pure in all of this.

He appointed Filangeri minister. While waiting for the many reforms and concessions, which the new minister promised us, we have been granted an amnesty, amnesty for what! Hearings and judgements.

Although not agreeable to Cavour or Garibaldi, the Peace of Villafranca, the Austrian loss of Lombardy, and the success of Victor Emmanuel were celebrated by sympathizers in Naples. They hoped the triumph of Piedmont would encourage change in their kingdom. It was evident to all by the following spring that Francis II was his father's son. There were no substantive reforms and repression continued. In April a revolution in Palermo foreshadowed the crisis the monarchy desperately sought to avoid.

April 7, 1860
Official news of the revolution in Sicily claimed it had been suppressed but not suffocated …
Naples is quiet but the papers say a demonstration of eight thousand people is planned tonight for Naples.

---

3 This and following quotes are from Craxi, Bettino ed., *Anonimo napoletano: Garibaldi o La conquista delle Due Sicilie*

Garibaldi's entrance into Naples in September 1860 was received with enormous popular enthusiasm. Naples held a plebiscite on unification on November 7, after the battle of Volturno but before the surrender of Gaeta, which indicated that the people of Naples supported unification. However, this was merely a popular affirmation; the coronation, which took place after the Piedmontese/north Italian Parliament voted in favor of unification in February 1861, marked the official unification. (Library of Congress)

April 26, 1860
On Saturday April 14 at Palermo there were
thirty killed by gunfire. The next day, or the day
after there was a demonstration with cries of
"Long Live Victor Emmanuel," and this is not
accepted under Martial Law. Turning to Naples,
… an order was issued for the arrest of anyone
speaking of things concerning Sicily.

The king surrounded himself with military advisors and ministers drawn from the Army. They pressed the king to take a hard line toward insurrection. Francis II agreed, but failed to recognize that the dread of revolution could be overcome with sincere reforms along the line of his brother monarchs to the north. Even Pius IX had instituted reforms in the years after 1849. By relying on hard power to keep the population in check, particularly in

the cities, he tied down much of his army, and fed the agitation.

Gossip about Garibaldi's expedition reached Naples. These rumors appeared in the official newspaper. An enormous curiosity plagued the city that starved for information on his progress. The Bourbon regime promoted its own version of events, but conceded Garibaldi's victory at Calatafimi and confirmed fighting in Palermo ten days later. Francis approved a constitution shortly after the fall of Palermo. Yet the author of the journal remained suspicious of royal intentions. The political opposition in the capital used the fall of Palermo as an opportunity to challenge the king via legislative means.

By the end of July, Garibaldi's arrival at Messina was accompanied by speculation that he would cross into Naples. Not long after Garibaldi's landing on the mainland, partisan bands formed in and around the capital city. Their captains recruited men and distributed declarations of Garibaldi's impeding arrival. News of Garibaldi's landing was met with great enthusiasm in Naples according to the author. Increasing demonstrations, and the apprehension of Garibaldi, hindered the police from enforcing order. By August 28, the Royal Guard had departed the city and Naples was placed in a state of siege. The actions of the royal administration indicated a real fear of revolution from within, at the moment Garibaldi appeared at the gates.

September 6, 1860
Garibaldi is in Naples, and all the city
responded enthusiastically; but there is
moderation to our enthusiasm …

The author joined the celebration that followed. The streets of the city were lined with thousands of Italian flags with the Cross of Savoy. During Garibaldi's procession the crowds cheered, "Long Live Garibaldi, Long Live Victor Emmanuel, Long Live Italy." The personal account of these events is strewn with unmistakable references to the association between Garibaldi and

Victor Emmanuel. There is no confusion as to the relationship between them and the eventual union with the north. Of course, the *brigandaccio*, the civil war in the south, which developed in 1861 in opposition to Piedmont, was centered in the countryside. Naples largely supported the unification.

During his time in Naples Garibaldi promulgated a constitution that combined the stillborn Neapolitan charter of 1848 and the Piedmontese statutes of 1845. It was more than Francis had attempted a month earlier. The reforms pleased moderates, but Mazzini's arrival in the city caused them concern. There was little interest in forcing a republican revolution, particularly when the city was still in the throes of celebration after the flight of the king and the arrival of the great hero.

The author of the journal remarked that on October 6, 1860, three days after Garibaldi's victory on the Volturno, cries of "Death to Mazzini" were heard in the streets.

On November 7, 1860, after a Neopolitan plebiscite that affirmed the unification of north and south, Victor Emmanuel and Garibaldi appeared together in Naples, "the king in full dress uniform and Garibaldi in his red poncho and his old felt hat." Garibaldi addressed the crowds, proclaiming the results of the plebiscite and then announcing that he was returning to private life. The author remarked that while Garibaldi intended to return to Caprera, unification was incomplete without Venice and Rome.

From Villafranca to Gaeta

The Second War of Italian Unification ended
in stages. The war against Austria concluded
with the armistice at Villafranca, which was
followed by several months of negotiations in
Switzerland. Hostilities formally concluded in
November 1859 with the Treaty of Zurich. The
Garibaldinian campaign in the Kingdom of
the Two Sicilies, and Piedmontese operations
in the Papal States, ended with the fall of
Gaeta and the declaration of Victor Emmanuel
as King of Italy. In the months between Zurich
and Garibaldi's invasion of Sicily, the central
Italian duchies and Papal territories of the
Romagna and Legations united with Piedmont
to form the Kingdom of Italy.

From the Peace of Villafranca to the Treaty of Zurich

The results of the battle of Solferino did not
compel Franz Josef to seek peace terms. The
Austrian army was bloodied, but in good
order. The French and Piedmontese had
suffered gravely too. Franz Josef could have
withdrawn to the safety of the Quadrilateral,
as Radetzky had done in 1848. Although the
Piedmontese placed Peschiera under siege,
the lessons of 1848 made it clear that only
the fall of Mantua or Verona would have a
decisive impact. Napoleon Bonaparte spent
six months on the defensive in 1796, until
Mantua fell. Charles Albert's position before
Verona had been irrelevant with Mantua
securely in Austrian hands. The allied general
staffs understood this, and established
contingency plans in case the Austrians
abandoned Lombardy for the Quadrilateral.
They agreed that Mantua had to be taken if
the war moved into Venetia.

The decision to offer terms did not
originate in the Austrian camp, although
Franz Josef was pleased with the invitation.

Napoleon III concluded that the cost of the
war and the threat of a general European
conflict were too great to continue the
campaign. After the French army crossed the
Ticino into Lombardy, defeated the Austrians
at Magenta, and occupied Milan, a palpable
fear emerged in Berlin, London, and St
Petersburg. In the light of events, questions
emerged concerning Napoleon III's true
intentions. Former British foreign secretary
Lord Malmesbury wrote his successor Lord
Cowley in mid-June that the rapid progress
of the French army in Italy indicated that the
war might not have been accidental. This may
have bothered Derby's administration, but did
not concern Palmerston or his cabinet. What
moved the European capitals was the
mobilization of the Prussian and Federal
armies, and the potential of war between
France and the German Confederation.

Prince Wilhelm wanted to use the conflict
to leverage Austria out of the leadership of
the Confederation. At the end of May
Franz Josef offered Wilhelm command of
the Federal Army if he promptly mobilized.
The prince regent did nothing, but shortly
after Magenta he gave Moltke permission to
prepare an army of observation on the Rhine.
In a seemingly favorable turn of events
for Austria, Wilhelm decided on armed
mediation. He would offer his services to
settle the conflict, but failing Napoleon III's
agreement he would support Austria. More
bluster than bite, Wilhelm had no intention
of committing his state to war, largely
because the Russians and British opposed
the expansion of the conflict too. Prussian
envoys relayed to the capitals the prince's
desire to conclude the war peacefully.

Napoleon III had prepared for a potential
conflict with the German Confederation
prior to the outbreak of war, but did not
desire to fight Austria in Germany.

The French Armée d'Observation consisted of eight divisions spread from Lille to Lyon. The Federal Army had seven corps, but dispersed from Westphalia to Frankfurt to the upper Rhine. None were yet concentrated. To be sure, Prussian and Confederation mobilization did not include an Austrian contingent. They did not want to settle Austria's war in Italy on the Rhine. Nevertheless, General Fleury sought assurances from the Russian ambassador, Kiselev, in Paris that should a war break out with Prussia, Russia would provide material support to its French ally. Neither Kiselev nor Czar Alexander II had any such idea.

Napoleon III understood the situation quite well after Solferino. The Empress Eugenie and Count Walewski informed him of events in Germany. His army had fought two large battles, defeated the Austrians in both encounters and "liberated" Lombardy. His agreement with Victor Emmanuel and Cavour was only half fulfilled, but he would not sacrifice the advantages gained to pursue the war further. On July 4, Walewski informed the British that the French emperor intended to conclude a peace with Austria. On July 6, Fleury traveled incognito to Verona where he presented Franz Josef with a letter requesting an armistice.

On July 8, 1859, French and Austrian military representatives signed a ceasefire agreement. Three days later Napoleon III and Franz Josef met at Villafranca, and affirmed their personal desires to end the war. Direct negotiations were conducted between Prince Jérôme Napoleon and Franz Josef. Through his emissary, Napoleon III proposed the cession of Lombardy and the creation of an Italian Confederation under the honorary presidency of Pius IX. Franz Josef accepted the fate of Lombardy, but would only cede it to France as victor; what Napoleon did with it afterward was his business. The Austrian emperor further demanded the restoration of the royal houses to Tuscany and Modena. Parma was left to the Piedmontese.

Napoleon III informed King Victor Emmanuel II of the settlement by early afternoon, and sought the Italian monarch's understanding of the situation. The king, albeit disappointed at leaving Venetia in Austrian hands, clearly understood the greater crisis looming in Europe. A war between France and Germany over the Italian question might lead to the loss of everything. Lombardy and Parma were better than nothing, and it was more than his father had achieved.

Victor Emmanuel told Cavour about the armistice and the general agreement on the evening of July 11. Unlike the king, the prime minister raged at the "betrayal." He argued with Victor Emmanuel and tendered his resignation. Cavour however, did not remain silent and directed events from behind the scenes. Indeed, Cavour argued from "retirement" that France would never receive Nice and Savoy because it had abrogated its part of the bargain.

Parma, Modena, Tuscany, and the Papal Romagna and Legations had risen in revolt with the support of the French V Corps and then occupation by Piedmontese forces. Despite the agreement at Villafranca, the Piedmontese encouraged revolution in these regions. When French and Austrian representatives met in Zurich in September, the Italian duchies and half the Papal States were under the control of pro-Piedmontese revolutionaries. Napoleon III could do little to prevent it, and Franz Josef had no intention of returning to the path of war to prevent it.

Republican and moderate revolutionaries quibbled in Tuscany, Modena, and Parma over the direction of the revolutions. Luigi Farini was proclaimed Dictator of Modena and Parma, and Colonel Leonetto Cipriani ruled the Romagna. These men desired to see their states annexed by Piedmont, and maintained an administration that advocated such a course. Only in Tuscany was there a significant movement to retain independence from Piedmont, but there was little international support for it.

The Peace of Zurich was signed in November 1859, but did not resolve the issue of the duchies. The treaty affirmed the transfer of Lombardy to France, which then ceded it to Piedmont. The notion of an Italian confederation also faded in the negotiations and appeared as an idea of interest. When the treaty was signed on November 10 the Piedmontese had reduced all those issues that they had found offensive in the Villafranca accord to nothing of consequence in the formal treaty. This was an enormous victory for Victor Emmanuel and the emerging Kingdom of Italy.

Franz Josef did not interpret the treaty as a defeat. He was not pleased with the outcome of the war, but believed that international pressure had prevented Napoleon III from achieving his goals, and deterred him from future ambitions. The Austrian emperor told his friend and

Two weeks after the battle of Solferino Napoleon III and Franz Josef met to agree to terms ending the war of 1859. The specifics were addressed later that day by Prince Jérôme Napoleon and the Austrian emperor. (Anne S.K. Brown Military Collection, Brown University Library)

confidant Kempen that he considered Zurich a temporary agreement. He had every intention of revising the treaty and would seek the assistance of the King of the Two Sicilies. Of course, Garibaldi's campaign in 1860 prevented Franz Josef from pursuing that plan.

Cavour was never far from Italy, even when he traveled Europe. He continued to advise his successor, General Alfonso La Marmora, who served as the prime minister after Cavour's departure. Cavour also did much to advocate for a new Italy. In January 1860 King Victor Emmanuel invited Cavour to return to his post as prime minister. Cavour accepted and threw himself into his work. The prime minister moved swiftly to bring the duchies directly into Piedmont and worked with the pro-Piedmontese governments to effect plebiscites. During the month of March, under the watchful eyes of Piedmontese troops, Italians in Parma, Modena, Tuscany, and the

Legations voted on Piedmontese annexation. Cavour left nothing to chance, and it is clear that the election was not entirely honest. International support was needed to legitimize the expansion of the Piedmontese crown and while Britain found all of this favorable, Napoleon III demanded the cession of Nice and Savoy for his acquiescence.

The annexation of the central duchies and the Papal Romagna and Legations unified all of northern Italy except Venetia. Garibaldi was fuming at the cost. As a member of the new parliament, he railed against the abandonment of Nice, the city of his birth. Napoleon III had "betrayed" Italy by making peace, he argued, and Cavour was complicit. Garibaldi's anger, however, abated after he decided to go to Sicily. Victor Emmanuel and Cavour were pleased to back his expedition, but in the same manner as they had supported the revolutions in the central duchies.

The Papal Domains and the south

Garibaldi's expedition provided wonderful cover for Piedmontese plans. His raid at Talamone not only diverted attention from Sicily, but instilled dread in Pius IX, who believed that Rome was the intended target. Napoleon III also worried that Garibaldi wanted to strike at the seat of papal power as he had in 1849. The emperor also knew well Garibaldi's hostility toward him for 1849, Villafranca, and the transfer of Nice to France. French troops garrisoned Civitavecchia and Rome, but that would not deter the charismatic revolutionary. Napoleon III feared republicanism and Garibaldi represented the Mazzinians in his imagination. Of course, Mazzini had broken with Garibaldi in 1859 for openly recognizing Victor Emmanuel as the

Alfonso La Marmora was a leading military and political figure of the Risorgimento. An officer in the Piedmontese army, he served as a staff officer in 1848, and a senior officer in the Crimea. In 1859, he held post as Minister of War. He succeeded Cavour as Prime Minister, after the latter's death in 1862. In 1866, he bungled operations, which led to the defeat at Custozza. Flanked on either side by Generals Cialdini (right) and Fanti (left), they represent central figures in the Piedmontese military efforts to unify the Italian peninsula. (DeAgostini Picture Library/Scala, Florence)

Giuseppe Garibaldi and Victor Emmanuel II met at Teano on October 29, 1860. Their meeting unofficially established the unification of Italy. Garibaldi commanded the Southern Army, which joined with the Piedmontese marching from the north. (Mary Evans Picture Library)

future King of Italy. When during the raid on Talamone Garibaldi again proclaimed his actions to the Thousand in the name of Victor Emmanuel and Italy, a number of volunteers left the expedition, refusing to serve.

After the fall of Sicily and the march of the Garibaldini to Messina, Cavour and the Piedmontese king convinced Napoleon III that Garibaldi intended to take Rome after Naples. Garibaldi accommodated the arguments by making such pronouncements. Napoleon III, Cialdini, and Fanti met surreptitiously at Chambéry in Savoy in August. They convinced the French emperor that the only way to avoid a republican revolution in Rome was to pre-empt it by invading the Marche and Umbria. The Piedmontese Army would occupy these Papal provinces, securing them from a Mazzinian revolution. Napoleon III saw this

as a better security against revolution than what had occurred months earlier in the central duchies. He accepted the plan for invasion and annexation, but demanded that Cavour guarantee that Rome and its immediate region remain under Papal control.

Cavour's machinations worked well, and the campaign in the Marche and Umbria coincided with Garibaldi's conquest of Naples. After the battle of the Volturno, Cavour justified the movement of Piedmontese forces to the south after a revolutionary committee in Abruzzi requested assistance. The union of Piedmontese and Garibaldinian armies was complete. The unofficial unification of Italy can be dated to October 26, 1860, when Garibaldi and King Victor Emmanuel II shook hands at Teano. Shortly thereafter, the former Mazzinian hero of the Risorgimento returned to his island of Caprera. The official unification occurred on March 17, 1861, when Victor Emmanuel II, King of Piedmont–Sardinia was acclaimed Victor Emmanuel I, King of Italy by the new Italian Parliament.

Conclusion and consequences

The Kingdom of Italy

Cavour achieved his dream of a united Italy under the constitutional monarchy of the House of Savoy. The price in territory was the loss of Nice and Savoy, the hereditary lands of the dynasty, but the population of these was largely ethnic French, and therefore could be rationalized away. The failure to "liberate" Venetia from Austrian rule, and Rome from the papacy was troublesome, but the prime minister remained pleased with his work. The process did not develop as planned, but he succeeded in preventing republicans from co-opting his revolutions. To be sure, the unification of Italy was as much a conquest of the peninsula by the Kingdom of Piedmont–Sardinia as it was the victory of a "national" uprising.

Giuseppe Mazzini and his followers refused to recognize the legitimacy of the Kingdom of Italy. Carlo Cattaneo, a disciple, continued to rail against Victor Emmanuel's regime. The National Society had surpassed Mazzini's Party of Action for control of Italian revolutionaries. Much of the reason lay with the failures of Mazzinianism to provide tangible gains for Italy. Garibaldi had concluded that his former mentor was nothing more than an intellectual, incapable of making clear decisions during their time in Rome in 1849. Mazzini was the injured party, as Garibaldi straddled the bridge between republicanism and conservative constitutionalism, and thereby possessed what Mazzini lacked.

Prior to the union with Piedmont Garibaldi's dictatorship in Sicily and Naples served to defeat the Bourbon regime, but did not bring to the Sicilian and Neapolitan peasantry what they desired: a less intrusive central government, land, and lower taxes. The tens of thousands of Sicilians of the *squadre* did

General Enrico Cialdini participated in the revolution in Modena in 1831. He went into exile, fighting with other Italian expatriates in Portugal and Spain. He returned to Italy in 1848 and was commissioned in Victor Emmanuel's army. His 4th Division saw substantial combat during the first month of the war in 1859. Cialdini was a consummate military professional responsible for conducting operations against the rebels in southern Italy after unification. (Anne S.K. Brown Military Collection, Brown University Library)

not cross the Straits of Messina with Garibaldi. The thousands who flocked to Garibaldi during his march on Naples were raised in Calabria, but their desire to overthrow the Bourbon regime did not translate into support for unification with Piedmont.

The *brigandaccio*

Unlike popular response in Lombardy and central Italy, the unification of Italy was seen in the south as a war of conquest. Not long after Garibaldi's victory at Volturno, local peasant revolts, spurred by Bourbon agents, broke out. The regions that exhibited resistance to the new order had also been contentious toward the old regime. After Francis II surrendered at Gaeta, he called upon his subjects not to abandon the Bourbon cause. By 1862, disturbances in the countryside toward the Piedmontese administration and military occupation exploded into a virtual civil war in the south.

General Enrico Cialdini was given the responsibility of suppressing the *brigandaccio* – the war against brigands. The new Italian government considered the peasant unrest a reflection of both Bourbon sympathies and the backward nature of the people of the south. Regional tensions flared both in the rebellions and in the reaction to them. The tradition of resistance to central authority continued under new circumstances. The level of brutality was reminiscent of the San Fedesti revolt of 1799 and the Calabrian revolt of 1806. Sporadic fighting continued through much of the 1860s.

The Third War of Italian Unification, 1866

Neither Cavour nor Victor Emmanuel abandoned their desire to incorporate Rome and Venetia into the new kingdom. Cavour offered Cardinal Antonelli a personal bribe of 15 million lire to encourage Pius IX to accept annexation. The prime minister offered the Pope a free hand in religious affairs, if he would agree to a union with Italy. Victor Emmanuel followed the same course when he proposed to purchase Venetia from Franz Josef. In both events, neither Pius IX nor the Austrian emperor were willing to abandon their states.

The greatest shock came when Camillo Benso, Count of Cavour, died suddenly on June 6, 1860. He had fallen ill and never recovered. The loss of Cavour deprived Victor Emmanuel and the new kingdom of perhaps one of the three greatest diplomats of the 19th century, alongside Metternich and Bismarck. Cavour's ability to manipulate individuals and

parties in Italy and to play upon the European state system was unique. After his death Victor Emmanuel was ill served by his prime ministers. The relationship and stability built between Cavour and the king over a decade of service did not exist among Bettino Ricasoli, Urbano Ratazzi, Luigi Carlo Farini, Marco Minghetti, or Alfonso La Marmora, his successors between 1861 and 1866.

The Rome and Venetia questions dominated Italian policy through the 1860s. Negotiations with the papacy and Napoleon III were a regular feature of Italian diplomacy. In 1862, frustrated with a lack of movement on the Roman front, Victor Emmanuel appointed Urbano Ratazzi prime minister. Ratazzi thought well of Garibaldi and the two met to discuss options concerning Rome. Garibaldi understood these meetings to imply tacit approval if he raised volunteers and marched on the city. Ratazzi intended to repeat Cavour's strategy of using revolutionary threats as a rationale to deploy Italian troops to secure territory from radicals. If Garibaldi advanced on Rome, then Ratazzi could authorize the Italian troops to occupy the city to prevent its fall.

Garibaldi landed in Sicily in 1862 and quickly organized 3,000 volunteers for the project. He adopted the slogan, "Roma o Morte!" – Rome or Death! In August, almost precisely two years after his famous crossing, Garibaldi landed in Calabria and advanced north. At this moment, Napoleon III separately warned Ratazzi that any attack on the French garrison in Rome would be understood as an Italian plot. Franz Josef also informed the Italian government that the sovereignty of the papacy was unimpeachable. Ratazzi had overplayed his hand, and the French and Austrians demanded that the Italian Army prevent Garibaldi from reaching the city. On August 29, 1862, Italian troops under Cialdini engaged Garibaldi at Aspromonte. After a short firefight, Garibaldi was wounded and captured. If Victor Emmanuel's forces had failed to act, French intervention was assured.

The fate of Rome was put aside temporarily as events in Germany provided

new opportunities to address the Venetian question. Otto von Bismarck assumed his role as Chancellor of Prussia in 1861. His determination to challenge Austria was well known, and the new Italian government believed that Prussia could serve as a valuable ally against Austria. Moreover, Bismarck initially believed that Napoleon III would favor any challenge to Austria's position in Germany. Unfortunately, none of this manifested itself in 1864 when Bismarck took a different approach and made common cause with Austria in the German Confederation. The Danish War of 1864 temporarily established an Austro-Prussian military alliance. La Marmora, the new prime minister, was unaware that this represented a temporary expedient rather than a new course for Prussia.

Bismarck approached Napoleon III a year later to make serious proposals concerning an anti-Austrian alliance. He recommended that Italy be included, considering that it coveted Venetia. The French emperor agreed to Bismarck's proposals and encouraged Italo-Prussian dialogue. Military and diplomatic negotiations between Turin and

The Third War of Italian Unification in 1866 led to Italian annexation of Venetia. In 1859, the Second War succeeded in bringing Lombardy into the new state, but Venetia remained in Austrian hands. Prussia and Italy allied against Austria in 1866 and although the Austrian Army defeated the Italians at the second battle of Custozza, Prussia's victory over Austria at Königgrätz led to the surrender of Austria's Italian province to Prussia, which transferred it to its Italian ally. (De Agostini/Getty Images)

Berlin continued through the spring of 1866. In mid-April a military convention established that Italy would receive Venetia in the event of victory over Austria. When war came on June 19, La Marmora assumed command of Italian armies and Baron Ricasoli returned as prime minister.

The Austro-Prussian War of 1866 is understood in Italy as the Third War of Italian Unification. The Archduke Albrecht commanded the Austrian army in Venetia. It was outnumbered, but had a capable general and the strength of the Quadrilateral system. The Italian Army fielded 200,000 men, including a corps under Garibaldi that operated in the Alps. La Marmora led the main army on the Mincio and Cialdini a smaller one on the Po. The strategic position of Italian forces offered them all the opportunity for a quick victory. Yet the Italian Army was a relatively new creation.

The merging of the Piedmontese and Garibaldini in 1861 was only the first stage in the establishment of a national army. Over the next five years, the Army had to integrate the various regional armies and its officer corps. Equipment, training, and tactics had to be standardized, and the dominance of the Piedmontese generals in the new army accepted. All of this had yet to be achieved by the summer of 1866. Heroes of 1859 and 1860 commanded corps during this campaign, but, while familiar to the soldiers, they lacked the experience to direct large military formations.

Despite these shortcomings, the greatest problem experienced by the Italian Army was a lack of strategic and operational coordination between La Marmora and Cialdini. Personal animosity and rivalry fed into the issue, but La Marmora bears the brunt of criticism. The general lacked *coup d'œil* – a foresight for military operations based upon years of experience. His Austrian opponent did not. La Marmora proceeded across the Mincio without Cialdini's support, confident that his army on its own outnumbered the archduke's.

On June 24 the Austrians struck along the line from Sommacampagna to Custozza and west toward the Mincio. The second battle of Custozza was a hard-fought engagement that resulted in the abject defeat of La Marmora's army. The scattered Italian divisions crossed the Mincio and took a defensive posture. The Austrians were however in no position to pursue, especially with Cialdini's 80,000 men to the south. The war against Prussia fared much worse, and after the battle of Königgrätz on July 3 Austria's defeat was assured. In the peace settlement in October Austria handed Venetia to France, and left Napoleon III to determine its fate. The French emperor transferred the province to Italy. Rome, however, still eluded Victor Emmanuel, Garibaldi, and the nationalists.

The Fourth War of Italian Unification, 1870

The political victory of 1866 created a second opportunity to strike at Rome. While Napoleon III contended with Prussia's looming military power, Ratazzi – having again returned as prime minister – believed that Garibaldi might succeed in 1867 where he had failed in 1862. This was a foolhardy notion. Once more, Garibaldi raised volunteers, but pressure from the French emperor, and some in Victor Emmanuel's cabinet led to his deportation to Caprera. Garibaldi and his supporters continued their recruitment. He arrived in Florence in October 1867 and led an

Archduke Albrecht was the son of the famed Austrian prince and military commander the Archduke Karl. Albrecht learned his professionalism and dedication to the Imperial-Royal Army through his father's example. He served as a special envoy for the Emperor Franz Josef in 1859, traveling to Berlin to determine Prussia's stance on the impending conflict with France. Albrecht commanded the Austrian army in Italy in 1866 and defeated the Italians at the second battle of Custozza. (© Bettmann/Corbis)

expedition to Rome. Napoleon III dispatched forces from Toulon to aid Papal troops. On November 3 Garibaldi fought a combined Papal-French army at Mentana. His forces were overwhelmed and Garibaldi captured.

The defeat at Mentana prevented the immediate seizure of the city, but in this attempt the Italian government was clearly complicit. Two years later, war between Prussia and France appeared a distinct reality, and the French emperor sought Italian military assistance. Negotiations between Napoleon III and Luigi Menebrea, the Italian prime minister, faltered on the Roman question. If France wanted a military alliance with Italy, Napoleon III must accept Italian annexation of Rome. Unwilling to consent, the French went to war with Prussia in July 1870. Victor Emmanuel, his cabinet, and the Italian parliament would not risk a formal assault on Rome even after the French garrison had withdrawn from the city. It was only after the defeat of the French Army at Sedan, and the revolution in Paris that removed the imperial regime, that a decision was made.

General Raffaele Cadorna (formerly the young officer who led the advanced guard at San Martino) led his Italian corps to the gates of Rome in mid-September. On September 20, Italian artillery opened fire on the walls near the Porta Pia. Within 30 minutes a breach was effected and Italian troops entered the city. General Hermann Kanzler, commander of the Papal forces in Rome, had received orders from Pius IX to defend the city until the walls were breached. At that time, Kanzler was authorized to offer terms of surrender. Pius IX had resigned himself to the capture of his city and the end of more than 1,000 years of temporal power of the papacy.

The Risorgimento in retrospect

The unification of Italy required four wars of varying dimensions to finally achieve the goals of both its liberal and conservative advocates. The traditional perspective of the Risorgimento revolved around the roles of "great men" such as Mazzini, Garibaldi, Cavour, and Victor Emmanuel. It is unclear if unification would have occurred without them. The "historians of the left" in Italy challenged the concept of national unification, referring to the Risorgimento and the process of unification as a bourgeois enterprise, without regard to the peasantry or the urban poor. There is some truth to their argument that unification was achieved by conquest rather than revolution, but revolutions did play a part. Revolutions in the central duchies provided Cavour with the opportunity to annex central Italy. Tuscans wanted to retain their independence after the grand duke fled, but those in Parma, Modena, and Lombardy welcomed the union with Piedmont. The responses of Neapolitans and Sicilians varied, but many did not approve of the military and political dominance of the north. Regionalism remains an issue of concern in modern Italy. Nonetheless, while the rural population may not have supported unification at that moment, the concept of "Italy" was gradually accepted.

After the fall of Rome, the Kingdom of Italy became one of six major European powers. Its prime ministers and leading politicians drew on their personal actions during the wars of unification to legitimize their political careers and commitment to Italy as a nation. Italy among the great powers attempted to shape its own course during the following years. Austria, the historic enemy, became an ally in 1882, when Italy joined the Triple Alliance. France, which had provided Italian national aspirations with men, money, and *matériel*, became a rival power. The greatest challenges to unification had been the creation of a clear national identity, and the development of the Italian kingdom into a modern industrial society.

Select bibliography

Archival sources

Austria, Vienna, Haus-Hof und Kriegsarchiv:
AFA 1859, *Armee unter Gyulai*

France, Château de Vincennes, Archives de la Marine, Fonds modernes, Série BB Service Général:
BB3 Correspondance général, Marseille, Alger, Colonies, 1859
BB5 Armements (1778–1920)

France, Château de Vincennes, Service historique de l'armée du terre, Série G3–G5:
G3 Correspondance, Armée d'Italie 1859

Italy, Rome, Archivio dell'Ufficio Storico dello Stato Maggiore dell'Esercito:
G-3 *Campagna* 1860–61
G-17 *Campagna* 1859
G-25 *Studi Tecnici*

Italy, Rome, Archivio della Marina Militare:
Titolario 1, *Documentazione dall'anno 1793 al 1914*, Busta 82, Fasc. 1

Printed sources

Abba, Giuseppe Cesare, *The Diary of One of Garibaldi's Thousand*, Oxford: Oxford University Press, 1962.

Agrati, Carlo, *I Mille nella storia e nella leggenda*, Milan: Mondadori, 1933.

Ales, Stefano, *Dall'Armata Sarda all'Esercito Italiano, 1843–1861*, Rome: USSME, 1990.

Alvarez, David, *The Pope's Soldiers: A Military History of the Vatican*, Lawrence, KS: University Press of Kansas, 2011.

Bapst, Germain, *Le Maréchal Canrobert: souvenirs d'un siècle*, Paris: E. Plon, 1904.

Battesti, Michele, *La Marine De Napoléon III: Une politique navale. Thesé de doctorat d'histoire* 2 vols, Paris: Service historique de la marine, 1997.

Beccaria, Auguste, "Lo sbarco francese a Genova 1859," *Rassegna storica nel Risorgimento* XII, 2(1925): 413–18.

Blumberg, Arnold, *A Carefully Planned Accident: The Italian War of 1859*, Cranbury, NJ: Associated University Presses, 1990.

Chiala, Luigi, ed., *Lettere edite ed inedite di Camillo Cavour*, Turin: Roux et Favale, 1884.

Coppa, Frank, *The Origins of the Italian Wars of Independence*, London: Longman, 1992.

Craxi, Bettino ed., *Anonimo napoletano: Garibaldi o La conquista delle Due Sicile*, Palermo: Sellerio editore, 1996.

Dépôt de la guerre, *La campagne de Napoleon III en Italie*, 3rd edition, Paris: Imprimerie Imperiale, 1865.

Di Lauro, Ferdinando, *1859: L'Armata Sarda a San Martino*, Rome: USSME, 2010.

Gabrièle, Mariano, *Sicilia 1860 da Marsala allo Stretto*, Rome: Ufficio Storico dell Marina Militare, 1991.

K. u. K. Generalstabes, *Der Krieg in Italien 1859*, 3 vols, Vienna: K. u. K. Generalstabes-Bureau für Kriegsgeschichte, 1872–1876.

Leonardis, Massimo de, *Epistolario di Giuseppe Garibaldi, Vol. V: 1860*, Rome: Istituto per la storia del Risorgimento italiano, 1988.

Moltke, Helmuth von, *La campagne d'Italie en 1859*, Paris: J. Dumaine, 1862.

Nava, Luigi, *L'Armata Sarda nella Giornata del 24 Giugno 1859*, Rome: Enrico Voghera, 1907.

Paoletti, Ciro, *Capitani di Casa Savoia*, Rome: USSME, 2007.

Paoletti, Ciro, *Gli Italiani in Armi: Cinque secoli di storia militare nazionale, 1494-2000*, Rome: USSME, 2001.

Pieri, Piero, *Storia militare del Risorgimento: Guerre e insurrezioni*, Turin: Einaudi, 1962.

Poplimont, Charles, *Lettres sur la campagne en 1859 Italie*, Paris: Tanera, 1860.

Redlich, Joseph, *Emperor Francis Joseph of Austria*, New York, NY: Macmillan, 1929.

Rothenberg, Gunther E., *The Army of Francis Joseph*, West Lafayette, IN: Purdue University Press, 1976.

Schmidt-Brentano, Antonio, *Die Armee in Österreich: Militär, Staat und Gesellschaft 1848–1867*, Boppard am Rhein: Harald Boldt, 1975.

Smith, Denis Mack, *Cavour and Garibaldi, 1860: A Study on Political Conflict*, Cambridge: Cambridge University Press, 1954.

Sondhaus, Lawrence, *The Habsburg Empire and the Sea: Austrian Naval Policy, 1797-1866*, West Lafayette, IN: Purdue University Press, 1989.

Thurston, G.J., "The Italian War of 1859 and The Reorientation of Russian Foreign Policy," *The Historical Journal*, 20, 1(1977): 121–44.

Ufficio Storico Stato Maggiore dell'Esercito, *il Generale Giuseppe Garibaldi*, Rome: USSME, 2007.

Ufficio Storico Stato Maggiore dell'Esercito, *L'assedio di Gaeta e gli avvenimenti militari del 1860–61 nell'Italia meridionale*, Rome: USSME, 2010.

Ufficio Storico Stato Maggiore dell'Esercito, *La Guerra del 1859*, 5 vols, Rome: Comando del Corpo di Stato Maggiore, 1910–1912.

Wawro, Geoffrey, *The Austro-Prussian War: Austria's War with Prussia and Italy in 1866*, Cambridge: Cambridge University Press, 1996.

Wingate, Andrew, "Railway Building in Italy before Unification," *Center for the Advanced Study of Italian Society Occasional Paper No. 3*, Reading: University of Reading, 1970.

Index

Figures in **bold** refer to illustrations

Abbiategrasso 44, 46, 51
Albrecht, the Archduke 75, 89, **90**
Alessandria 29, **29**, 37, 39, 40, 41, 42
Alexander II, Czar 31, 74, 76–7, 78, 83
Alps (the), operations in 42, **42**, 89
Ancona, siege of 65, 66–7
Austrian Empire
  decline of economy/power 9, 27, 30, 78
  diplomatic isolation of 74–8, 89, **89**
  goaded into war 7, 23, **23**, 24, 28, 29, 30, 31–2,
    34, 52, 74, 82
  revolution in 9, 14, 15, 25
Austrian 1st Army 51, 52, 53
Austrian 2nd Army 35, 39, **90**
  command of 25, 34, 51, 77, 89, **90**
  deployment and action 12, 13, 14, **15**, **16**, 17, **21**, 22,
    25, 26, **26**, **27**, 30, **32**, 35, 36, 37, **37**, 38, 39, 40,
    41, **41**, 42, **42**, 43, **43**, 44, 45, 46, **46**, 47, 48, 50,
    51, 52, 53, **53**, 54, 55, **55**, 56, 57, **57**, **58**, 77, **82**,
    89, **89**, 90
  quelling of revolution 14, **15**, 16–17
  reform and modernization of 25, 26
  weaponry: artillery 26, **26**, 55, 57; rifles 26

Benedek, Feldm'll Lt Ludwig von 41; **41**, 52, 55, 57
Bismarck, Chancellor Otto von 74, 77, 88, 89
Bixio, Nino 61, 62, 63, 69, 71, 72
Bosco, Colonel 63, 64, **64**
Brescia **51**, 54
brigandaccio (the) 81, 87–8, **87**
Buffalora, fighting at 47–8, **47**, 50
Buol, Count Karl von 75, 76

Cacciatore delle Alpi 39, 42–3, **42**, 54, 59, 61
Cadorna, General Raffaele 54, 55, 91
Calabria, Garibaldi lands in 87, 88
Calatafimi, battle of (1860) 61–2, 72, 80
Campo di Medole, fight for 52, 53–4
Canrobert, Marshal François Certain 36, 37, **38**, 41–2,
    43, **44**, 47, 48, 50, 53
Capua garrison, fight for 67, 69, 70
Carbonari revolutionary movement 10, 13–14
Casale fortifications 29, 37, 41, 42
Caserta, armed forces at 69, 70
Cassano **34**
Castelfidardo, battle of (1860) 22, 66
Castiglione 53, 54
Cavour, Prime Minister Camillo di 10, 22, 28, 65
  as advocate for unification 9, 27, 28, 74, 83, 84–5,
    87, 88, 91
  death of **85**, 88
  dismay at British diplomacy 22, 32, 78

fear of republican revolution 28, 51, 91
  and Garibaldi 28, 39, 59, 65, 73, 85
  goads Austria into war 23, 24, 28, 29, 30
  and King Victor Emmanuel II 83, 88
  and Napoleon III 24, 28, 31, 65, 83, 86
Cavriana, fight for 53, 54, 58
Charles Albert, King of Piedmont–Sardinia 14, 15–16,
    15, **16**, 17, 18, 19, **19**, 22, 35, 38, 58, 82
Cialdini, General Enrico **21**, 22, 41, 42, **42**, 43, **43**, 44,
    54, 66–7, 70, **85**, 86, **87**, 88, **89**–90
Clam Gallas, Feldm'll Lt 44, 50, 53
Cosenz, Enrico 61, 63, 64
Crimean War 23, 24, 25, 31, 77
Cucchiari, General Domenico 54, 55, 57
Custozza, battles of **16**, 19, 25, **85**, **89**, 90

d'Hilliers, Marshal Baraguey 36, 39, 40, 42, 53
Della Rocca, General 65, 66, 67, 70
Durando, General Giovanni 17, 18, 22, 23, 37, 43,
    54, 57

Fanti, General Manfredo 22, 42, 47, 48, 50, 51, 54, 57,
    65, 67, **85**, 86
Federal Army **41**, 75, 82, 83
Federati revolutionary movement 13
Ferdinand II, King of the Two Sicilies 13, 17, 19, 79, 84
Ferdinand IV, King of Naples 13, 14
Fleury, General Émile 31, 58, 83
Forey, General **12**, **37**, 39, 40, 53
France
  economic/military power of 78
  political rule of 23–5, **23**
  Second French Empire 22, 23, **23**
  Second Republic 22, 23, **23**
Francis II, King of Naples 27, 28, 63, 65, **69**, 79, 80,
    81, 88
Franco-Piedmontese Army 34–5, **34**, 38, 39–40, 42–4,
    42, **44**, 46–8, **48**, 51, 52, 77
Franz Josef, Emperor of Austria 44, 77, **90**
  as commander 25, 51, 52, 54, 57, 77, 82
  desire to expand war beyond Italy 74, 75, 76
  goaded into war 32, 36, 52, 74, 78
  peace with France 58, **76**, 82, 83, 84, **84**
French Armée d'Italie 35, 78
  deployment and action 12, **12**, 23, **27**, 31, **31**, 34, **34**,
    35, 36–7, **38**, 39, 40, 41–2, 43, 44, **44**, 45, 46, 47,
    47, 48, 50–1, **50**, 52, **52**, 53–4, **54**, 57, 58, 82, 83,
    85, 91
  transport of 34–5, **34**, 36, **38**, 40, 42
  weaponry 24–5: artillery **26**
French Navy 31, 35, 36, 52, 78

Gaeta, siege of 65, 67, **68**, **69**, 70, 82, 88
Garibaldi, Giuseppe 18, 19, 71–2, 81, 88

"betrayal" by Napoleon III 58–9, 85
British support for 60, **62**, 63, 78
and Cavour 28, 29, 39, 59, 65, 73, 85, 86
as Mazzinian radical 13, 29, 59, 85–6, 87
retirement to Caprera 70, 81, 86, 90
service in Piedmontese Army 39, 58
support for King Victor Emmanuel II 29, 39, 59, 70,
    73, 79, 85–6, **86**
Genoa, troops assemble at **29**, 35, 36, 37, 38, **39**, 52,
    59, 60, 65, 71
German Confederation 27, 32, 36, 41, 74–5, 89
Germany 74, 75, 83, 88–9
Great Britain
    diplomacy of 22, 23, 24, 31, 32, 74, 78
    naval support 60, 61, **61**, 62, **62**, 63, 78
Grünne, Feldm'll Lt Karl Ludwig Count 25–6, 30, 34,
    36, **41**, 75
Gyulai, Feldzeugmeister Franz 25, 36, 37, 38, 39, 40, 41,
    41, 42, 43, 44, **45**, 46, 47, 50, 51

Hess, Feldm'll Heinrich Baron von 30, 34, 36, **41**, 44,
    50, 58, 75
Hübner, Baron 29, 30

Italian Army, deployment and action 89, 90, 91
Italy (Kingdom of)
    achievement/declaration of 7, 87
    composition of (independent states) 7, **8**, 82
    date of unification 86, **86**
    as major European power 78, **89**, 91
    regional opposition to concept 79, 87–8, **87**

Karl, the Archduke 75, **90**
Königgrätz, battle of (1866) **89**, 90
Kuhn von Kuhnenfeld, Colonel Franz 34, 44, 46

La Farina, Giuseppe 28, 63, 65
La Marmora, General Alfonso 22, **22**, 23, 29–30, 35, 37,
    39, 40, 84, **85**, 88, 89, 90
La Masa, Giuseppe 59, 61, 62
La Motterouge, General 47, 48, 50, 53
Lamoricière, General 65, 66, 67
Liechtenstein, Feldm'll Lt Eduard Prince von 41, 48
Lombardy–Venetia (Kingdom of) 7, **8**, 17, 38
    annexation and unification of 9, 28, 83, **89**, 91
    Austrian control of 7, 9, 14, 17–19, 22, 25, 26, 28,
        30, 44, 82
    fighting for 14, 15–18, **16**, 28, 40, **42**, **51**, 52, 77, 79,
        82, 83
Lomellina, fighting in 35, 36, 37, 40, **42**, 43, 45

MacMahon, General **31**, 42, 43, **45**, 47, **47**, 48, 50,
    51, 53
Maddaloni, fighting at 67, 69, 70
Madonna della Scoperta 52, 53, **53**, 54, 57
Magenta, battle of (1859) **24–5**, **27**, **31**, 38, 44, **45**,
    46–8, 50–1, **50**, 54, 77, **82**
Mantua fortress 17, 18, 19, 58, 81
Marche (the), annexation of 65, 67, 86
Mazzini, Giuseppe 10, **13**, 14, 19, 28, 29, 81, 85–6,
    87, 91
Mazzinians 10, **13**, 14, 21, 22, 23, 28, 59

Mechel, Colonel von 27, 61, 62, 70
Medici, Giacome 61, 63, 64, 69, 70, 73
Mensdorff, Feldm'll Lt 44, 46, 50, 51, 53
Mentana, battle of the (1867) 79, 91
Messina, siege of 26, 59, 63, 64, 67, 80, 86
Metternich, Feldm'll Clemens von 13, 14, 25, 74, 88
Milan, fight for 14, **15**, 17, 18, 19, 26, 43, 44, 46, 47,
    51, **51**, 52, **72**, 82
Milazzo, battle of (1860) 63–4, **64**
Milbiz, General 69, 70
Modena (Duchy of) 7, **8**, 28, 51
    annexation and unification of 19, 84–5, 91
    support for revolution in 13, 14, 83
Mollard General 43, 54, 55, 57
Montebello, battle of **12**, 34, **37**, 39, 40–1, 44
Mortara 38, 41, 42, 43
Mundy, Admiral 60, **62**, 63, 66, 78

Naples (Kingdom of) 7, 59, 63
    Austrian acquisition of 7, 13–14
    civil unrest in 13, 14, 79–81, 87, 91
    Garibaldi conquers 64, 65, 78, 79, 80–1, **80**, 86, 87
Napoleon, Prince Jérôme 28, 29, 39, 51, 77, 83, **84**
Napoleon III, Emperor of the French 19–20, 22, 23, **23**,
    24, 28, 39, 46, 50, 75, 77, 82
    agreement with Cavour 27, 28, 65, 83
    attempt to kill 28
    as diplomat 23, 27, 28, 29, 30, 31, 32, 34, 39, 58,
        65, 74, 76–7, **76**, 82, 83, **84**, 85, 88
    enters Milan 51, **51**
    and the Italian question 24, 28, 85, 86, 88, 91
    as military commander 31, 32, 40, 47, 48, 53,
        57, 90
    President of the Second Republic 22, 23, **23**
National Society 27, 28, 59, 63, 87
Neapolitan Army
    deployment and action 17, 26, 59, **60**, 61, 62, **62**, 63,
        64, **64**, 67, **67**, 69, 70, 72
Neapolitan Navy 26, 60–1, 62, 65, 70, **73**
Nice (County of) 9, 28, 83, 85, 89
Niel, General Adolphe 29, 31, **38**, 41–2, 43, 47, 48, 50,
    53–4, **58**
Novara, battle of (1849) **16**, 35, 44, 48

Orsini, Felice 28

Palermo see under Sicily
Palestro, battle of (1859) **21**, 34, 41, 42–3, **42**, **43**, **44**,
    46, 54
Papal Army 17, 18, **22**, 65, 66, 67, 91
Papal States/territories 7, **8**
    annexation of 9, 65, 67, 82, 85
    invasion of 7, 26, 51, 65–7, 82
    revolution in 14, 83
Parma (Duchy of) 7, **8**, 28, 51
    annexation and unification of 19, 28, 71, 83,
        84–5, 91
    revolution in 13, 14, 51, 83
Pavia 38, 39, 43, 44, 51
Peace of: Olmütz (1850) 74; Villafranca (1859) 58, 76,
    78, 79, 82; Zurich (1859) 83–4
Persano, Admiral 59, 63, 66

Perugia and Pesaro, threats to 66
Peschiera fortress 18, 58, 82
Piacenza, fall of 38, 39, 40, 41, 44, 51
Piedmontese Army 17, 35, 37, 64, 65, **85**
    deployment and action 18, 19, **21**, 22, 34, 35, 36, 37,
        37, 40, 41–2, **42**, 43, **43**, 44, **44**, 47, 48, 50–1, **53**,
        54–5, **56**, 57, **57**, 58, 65, 66, 67, **68**, **69**, 70, 89, 82,
        86, **87**
    mobilization for war 22, 29–30, 36, 52
    Southern Army joins 64, 70, **86**
    weaponry: artillery **22**, 23, **26**, 57, 65
Piedmontese Navy, deployment and action 14, 26, 36, 59,
    63, 64, 66, 67, **69**
Piedmont–Sardinia (Kingdom of) 7, 8–9, **8**
    annexation and unification 9, 10, **80**, 91
    Austrian invasion of 14, 77
    economic development in 22, 27, **30**
    as part of the new Italy **80**, 89
    post-war changes in 21–3
    revolution in 13, 14
Pius IX, Pope **10**, 14–15, 17, 18, 19, 26, 65, 67, 80, 83,
    85, 88, 91
princes, role of in politics 8–9, 18
Prussia 74–5, 82–3, **89**, **90**, 91
Prussian Army 75, 76, 82, 89, 90, **90**, 91

Radetzky von Radetz, Feldm'll Josef 15, **15**, 16, **16**,
    17–19, **17**, 25, 35, **41**, 43, 51, 55, 82
Ratazzi, Prime Minister Urbano 88, 90–1
Rechberg, Count Bernard 74–5, 76
Ricasoli, Prime Minister Baron Bettino 88, 89
Risorgimento Italy, composition of **8**, 10
Rivendite revolutionary movement 13
Romagna and Papal Legations 28, 82, 83
Rome, attempts to incorporate **10**, 14–15, 19, 23, 25, 59,
    65, 70, 85, 86, 88, 90–1
Russia 23, 24, 31, 76–7, 83

San Fermo, fighting at 42, 54
San Martino, battle of (1859) **41**, 51, 52, 54, 55, **56**,
    57, **57**
Santa Maria, fighting at 69, 70
Savoy (Duchy of) 7, 9, 28, 35, 65, 83, 85, 87
Schwarzenberg, Feldm'll Lt Edmund Prince von 41, 46, 50
Sicily
    fight for Palermo 26, 59, 60, 61, 62–3, **62**, **63**, 72–3,
        73, 78, 79, 80
    Garibaldi's conquest of 7, 26, 27, 58–60, **60**, 61, **61**,
        62–3, **62**, 64, **64**, 69–70, 71, 72–3, **73**, 78, 80,
        87, 88
    revolution in 14, 26, 59, 62, **63**, 79, 80, 87
    volunteer fighters (*squadre*) 61, 62, 63, 64, 71, 72,
        72, 87
Siracusa 26, 59, 61, 63
Solferino, battle of (1859) **24–5**, **26**, 31, 34, **49**, 51–4,
    52, **53**, **54**, 55, 82

Southern Army **86**: deployment and action 16, 61, 63,
    64, 67, **67**, 69–70, 71, 72, 73
Stadion, Feldm'll Lt Count Rudolph Philipp 40, 41, 46,
    50, 53, **53**, 54, 57

Talamone, Garibaldi's raid on 60, 85, 86
'The Thousand' (*I Mille*)
    campaigns: Sicily 58, 59–60, **60**, 61, **61**, 62, 71–3, 86;
        Varese 42–3, **42**
    recruitment and volunteers 29, 42–3, **42**, 58, 59, 61,
        62, 63, 64, 71–3, **72**, 86
Toulon 31, 35, 36, 91
transport: rail 22, 26, **29**, **30**, 34–5, **34**, 36, **38**, 41–2, 48,
    52, 54; ship 34–5, **34**, 36, 38, **39**, 52, 59, 60, **61**,
    66, 71
Treaty of Paris (1856) 77
Treaty of Zurich (1859) 78, 82, 84
Turbigo 46, 47, 48
Turin 29, **29**, 34, 35, 37, 38, 52
Türr, General Stefan 16, 61, 63, 70, 73
Tuscany (Grand Duchy of) 7, 8, **8**, 9, 28
    annexation of 9, 28, 84–5
    military occupation of 39, 65, 83
    desire for independence 13, 14, 51, 83, 91
Two Sicilies (Kingdom of the) 7, **8**, 26–7, 70
    Garibaldi's campaign in 58, 59, 82
    protection of the monarchy 26, 27
    revolution in 26, 28, 79–80

Umbria, annexation of 65, 67, 86
Urban, Feldm'll Lt Karl 40, 41, 42

Varese, battle of (1859) 42–3, **42**, **72**
Venice 14, 17, 26
Vercelli **34**, 37, 38, 39, 41, 44
    military forces at **21**, 37, 38, **42**, 43, 48
Verona 15, **17**, 18, 19, 25, 51, 58, 82, 83
Victor Emmanuel II, King of Piedmont–Sardinia 7, **9**, 39,
    40, 41, 54, 70, 81, 86, 87
    antipathy toward Austria 22, 32, 36
    as military leader 29, 37, 43, **46**, 51, **51**, 57
    proclaimed Victor Emmanuel I, King of Italy 14, 63,
        70, 82, 85–6
    relationship with Garibaldi 39, 59, 64, 65, 69,
        70, 73, 79, 85, 86, **86**, 88
    relationship with Cavour 82, 83, 88
Volturno, battle of the (1860) 65, 67, **67**, 69–70,
    69, 73

Walewski, Count 31, 77, 83
Wilhelm, Prince Regent of Prussia 75, 76, 82
Wimpffen, Feldzeugmeister Count 51, 52

Young Italy (*Giovane Italia*) **13**, 14, 23

Zobel, Feldm'll Lt Johann Baron 41, 43, **46**